Sundays with Scottie

Sundays with Scottie

Milton Jones

LEAFWOOD
PUBLISHERS

Sundays with Scottie
published by Leafwood Publishers

Copyright © 2003 by Milton Jones

ISBN 0-9728425-4-3
Printed in the United States of America

Cover design by Rick Gibson

For information:
Leafwood Publishers
1648 Campus Court
Abilene, Texas 79601
1-877-816-4455 (toll free)

Visit our website: www.leafwoodpublishers.com

05 06 07 08 / 8 7 6 5 4 3 2

To Mike Dahlager

Thanks for your gift of giving me a hard time.
You always keep me from
becoming too important.
And you consistently bring laughter
into my life when I least expect it.

Glad
Cheerful
Overjoyed
Working
God
Art

—Scott Callis

Contents

Introduction

*S*undays with Scottie. It sounds like a rip off of *Tuesdays with Morrie*. I guess in a way it is. I am very thankful to Mitch Albom for his wonderful book where he tells the story of his professor, Morrie Schwarz. Albom's Tuesday visits to his mentor at the end of his life prompted me to examine a weekly visit in my life.

I read *Tuesdays with Morrie* shortly after the death of Scottie Callis. I had been with Scottie every Sunday for over two decades. That book encouraged me to go back and rethink all that I had experienced in this relationship. I would like to thank Mitch Albom for giving me the idea to examine and cherish a past friendship.

I could have called the book *Everything I Ever Needed for Life I Learned from a Guy with Cerebral Palsy*. And that would be true. Scottie defined for me what was important in life. I get too busy. I get too stressed. I am too materialistic. I am too smart. I am too important. And Scottie taught me that what I too often take pride in and what is truly important might be two different things.

I hope this book will cause you to understand people who have CP better. Maybe it will cause you to make a friend with someone who is different from you. I certainly hope it honors all my friends with CP, especially Mike Dahlager, Ila Mae Morgan, and Andy Vorpahl.

Milton Jones

C|P

"What's wrong with Scottie?" That was always the first question. And the first answer was always the same: "CP."

Certainly there are other answers, but they are more obvious. Scottie couldn't walk, at least not like the rest of us. He launched himself forward on a couple of crutches and dragged his feet behind him. And he always had his shoes on the wrong feet. Who knows why? But he consistently did it. He got it wrong every single time.

And Scottie couldn't talk. Well, he could, but you just couldn't understand him. You could learn to understand him, but it took effort. Well, actually, I take that back—he was understandable most of the time when he screamed something out in the middle of one of my sermons. But on other occasions, Scottie would have to repeat himself half a dozen times before you'd get what he was saying.

And Scottie was short, so short that you could simply look right over him if you were not careful. And he tended to have an otherworldly look about him, a wildness in his countenance. You would swear that he must have been a creation of Maurice Sendak and sent from *Where The Wild Things Are.*

Countless other things were wrong with Scottie once you started looking. But CP is still the answer you'd always hear. Scottie had cerebral palsy, a malady to summarize his life. A category to box him in. A designation to define him as different. A pigeonhole that kept people from treating him like everyone else.

Cerebral palsy (CP for short) is a condition that affects thousands of babies and children every year. It is not contagious, but it certainly leads to a very difficult life. "Cerebral" means having to do with the brain. "Palsy" means a weakness or problem in the way a person moves or the way he positions the body. Someone with CP usually has trouble controlling his muscles. In most people our brains tell the rest of our body exactly what to do and when to do it. However, since CP affects the brain, a person with cerebral palsy may not be able to walk, talk, eat, or move in the same way other people do.

There are three types of CP: spastic, athetoid, and ataxic. The most common is spastic where a person can't relax his muscles or the muscles become stiff. Athetoid CP affects a person's ability to control his muscles. This means that the arms or legs that are affected may flutter and move suddenly. Someone with ataxic CP has problems with balance and coordination.

CP comes in mild and severe cases depending upon how much of the body is affected. If both arms and legs are affected, a wheelchair may be necessary. If only the legs are affected, braces or crutches can help a person walk. If the part of the brain that controls speech is affected, a person will have trouble talking. And some people with CP can't talk at all.

No one knows for sure what causes CP. Injuries to the brain at birth often result in cerebral palsy. Premature babies or babies who need to be on a ventilator for a long time are more at risk for developing CP. But for most people who get CP, the problem develops in the brain before birth, and we simply don't know why.

There is no actual test to determine if a person has cerebral palsy. Doctors often test babies to rule out other diseases, but they must watch to see the development of the baby before CP is determined. A case of cerebral palsy can usually be diagnosed by the age of eighteen months. Unlike most children, babies with CP won't be able to sit up on their own by the age of six to seven months or walk by the age of ten to fourteen months. When a child doesn't sit up or walk when most other children do, doctors usually analyze them to find problems with muscle tone, movement, and reflexes.

CP does not get worse over time because the problem with the brain will not get worse as the child gets older. As an example, a child who has CP that affects only his legs will not develop CP in his arms or problems with his speech later on. The effect of CP on the arms or legs can get worse, however, and some can develop dislocated hips or curvature of the spine.

Therapy for CP is extremely important and specialized. Children with CP usually have physical, occupational, or speech therapy to help them develop skills like walking, sitting, swallowing, and using their hands. Communication tools like message boards and electronic talking machines are often used for those who can't talk. Medications are used to treat the seizures that may accompany CP and to relax the muscles. Some have surgery to keep their arms or legs straighter and more flexible.

People with CP may vary drastically in intellectual ability. Some have serious mental handicaps while others have a very high IQ. My friend Mike Dahlager has CP but has persevered through college. Ila Mae Morgan, in spite of her CP, has written books and created beautiful pieces of art. However, when it comes to Scottie, he was somewhat more mentally challenged. Scottie didn't have the highest intellect, but he could reason and surprise us with a highly developed sense of humor. He could walk only with crutches. And although it came with great difficulty, Scottie would get a lot of words out of his mouth. In fact, he would literally talk all day if you were patient enough to give him the time and to work at deciphering what he was saying.

In many ways, CP is a cruel disease. Most of my friends with CP are exceptional in observing and taking things in, but they just can't participate and respond as they desire. Scottie, however, didn't let the severe challenges of his life stop him. A life with CP was all he knew. It was his life. And no one was going to rob life from him. He may have had to participate more slowly, but he was certainly an example of the tortoise winning over the hare (if the race is measured by attitude, faith, and friends).

What's Right?

"What's wrong with Scottie?" That was simply the wrong question. The right question would be, "What's right with Scottie?" Because something was very right with Scottie, but you might have missed it if you focus only on what is wrong.

At first glance, Scottie had everything you don't want. He was small. He didn't have much going for him in the categories of power, sex appeal, or money. His IQ didn't top the charts. Win a beauty contest? Never. He was handicapped.

But on the other hand, Scottie had everything you want. He had those hidden attributes that nearly everyone is looking for but can't find. He had contentment. Maybe that's the greatest virtue manifested in Scottie's life. But he was also very happy. Smiles abounded on the face of Scott Callis. He had what he wanted: He had good friends. He was loved. He had faith. He found what he was looking for and had what everyone else wants but can't obtain.

So what was right with Scottie? I decided to look back at this friend of mine with whom I spent every Sunday for the last twenty years. I was his minister. I was his best friend. And I want to share with you what I gleaned from spending twenty years of Sundays with Scottie. If you get it, you will be happier. I think you will find contentment. Perhaps through this strange story of a small guy in Seattle, you too will find the hidden treasure that you have been seeking for so long. I'll try

16

to share these little lessons with you in the form of "Scottie-isms." They won't be hard to understand because Scott never was. These are the lessons learned from his life or mentioned from his mouth.

Whether from the story of Mother Teresa or the pen of Jimmy Carter, our age is being told over and over again that there is a greater happiness available to us when we live a simple life. Well, Scottie certainly lived life simply. But it was a good life. In fact, from my point of view, it was extraordinary.

Frankly, I don't know anyone who would have wanted to trade lives with him. No one wants CP. I can't think of anyone who would honestly say that he would take CP if he could only have what Scottie had. It's probably unfair to make anyone go through that postulation. But the truth is that what Scottie had and what you really want is available to you with or without CP.

Scottie's contentment was all about asking the right questions. Most of us have been asking the wrong questions in our minds. At least our starting questions have been incorrect. Scottie would have us reverse the usual order of our questions.

Scottie-ism #1
*Look for what's right before you
ever look for what's wrong.*

What's wrong? What's right? Which question comes to your mind first? People tended to ignore Scottie because their initial evaluation revolved around what was wrong with him rather than what was right. A failure in this first Scottie-ism could be a primary reason for not experiencing a happy life like Scottie's. You simply notice what is wrong before you ever see what is right.

Positive Thinking

Scottie was different. He noticed what was right first. If you first notice the good in people or situations, it affects your attitude. It makes life good. If you notice the bad first, it will probably skew your attitude toward the negative. Scottie was content because he saw what was good first. He concentrated on it. And his attitude was shaped by it.

It's all a mindset. The Apostle Paul put it this way: "Fix your thoughts on what is true and honorable and right. Think about things that are pure and lovely and admirable. Think about things that are excellent and worthy of praise" (Phil. 4:8, NLT).

This passage challenges us to consider what we think about. It's imperative to consider our thoughts because our minds are going to determine our anxiety level and the height of our contentment. According to Scottie's way of thinking, Philippians 4:8 is the beginning of our thought process, not the finale. What do you see first in people? Do you always notice what is wrong with them first? Or do you see the good in them?

I was frequently told the story of my grandmother, Nelly Francis, who always saw the good in everyone she met. It didn't matter how bad the person was—she tried to find some good. Her children kidded her that she would find something good in the devil. Her response was, "He does work very hard." She lived a happy and contented life under the very difficult circumstances of losing a husband to a tragic death and having to raise eleven children during the Depression by herself. How could anyone do that? And more importantly, how could anyone do it with a good attitude? Wouldn't you end up with a big case of the PLOMs (the poor little old me's)? How could you possibly be happy and contented when everything had fallen apart? She simply noticed the good around her first. She had eleven wonderful children whom she desperately loved and who loved her in return. All other situations, no matter how negative, had to be looked at later.

How do you see your situations? Whether at work, home, or school, do you tend to notice the negative first? It's like the nightly news. When is the last time the lead story focused on what was right in the world? If our discussion is on politics or the government, what comes out of our mouths first? Is it how we live in a wonderful country blessed with an amazing democratic process? No, we usually start with what's bugging us about our political system. And the sad part is that after we begin with the negative, we rarely follow it with anything positive. Typically, when the wrong comes first, the right is left out altogether.

Encouraging Words

You would think that churches would be different, wouldn't you? As a pastor, that's always been my dream. Church should be like a home on the range where "seldom is heard a discouraging word." But too often we bring this "what's wrong" view to church with us. We act as if we have been anointed with the gift of criticism. We pretend that God wants us to be the Siskels and Eberts of our congregation. We point out all the little things we don't like. And too often, these negative words are the first words out of our mouths. Jude called them "grumblers and fault-finders" (verse 16) and believed they would ruin the church. Wouldn't you love to be a part of a church (or any organization) where people first noticed what was right rather than what was wrong?

How many family problems could be solved with just this one Scottie-ism? Children slowly grow away from their parents if they know Mom's or Dad's first words

20

are going to point out what was wrong rather than what was right. Jim Morris, the subject of *The Rookie*, never gave up his dream of becoming a major league pitcher.[1] He finally reached his goal at the age of thirty-five. But throughout his whole ordeal, he was never able to shake the negative comments of his father. The lack of positive encouragement followed him decades after he had left home. When Jim was young, his dad hardly ever came to his ball games. He still remembers a rare day when his dad showed up at the park. The only voice he could hear from the stands was his father's "Throw strikes!" And instead of complimenting him between innings, his dad only told him what he was doing wrong. In one game, Jim struck out fourteen batters throwing a one hitter. In the same game, he also hit two home runs. But he struck out once, and that was all his dad mentioned.

What the most significant person in our lives thinks of us most often determines our self-esteem. If the people who are most important in our lives tell us of our value and worth to them, we usually have healthy self-images. If we don't get that positive feedback, we will probably get down on ourselves and seek positive strokes elsewhere in inappropriate ways. This seems to be especially true in marriages. Spouses who frequently hear affectionate words believe they are loved. With positive communication, marriages flourish and self-respect increases. When there is a lack of encouraging communication, self-worth can be diminished and love may be sought elsewhere.

Scottie wasn't married. He didn't have a spouse to communicate love and raise his self-worth. But Scottie had determined that God was going to be the most significant one in his life. And since God had first communicated to Scottie that He loved him, Scottie had a pretty healthy self-image. He had so many more reasons to be down in the dumps than most of us. He didn't have looks, money, power, or prestige. But he believed God loved him. That was the message he remembered first in the evaluation of his life, and it colored all the other situations he faced. When he looked at God, he saw what was right. And out of that first look, he could live with all the secondary wrongs.

When I start counting my blessings, I have found that there are a whole lot of things right in my life. When I evaluate my physical, financial, and spiritual blessings, it's as if I've won the cosmic lottery. How about you? What's right in your life? Think about it. Be thankful for it. Build upon it. And like Scottie, be content with it.

Why?

*H*ow in the world did Scottie get CP? That's a good question. *Why* in the world did Scottie get CP? That's a better question. It forces us to wrestle with matters of faith. It makes us question God. Did God do this? Why would a good God let something happen that seems so cruel?

Why? It's the question that little kids ask us over and over again. It is the question that we like to bury because we can't find good enough answers. It's basically the question the disciples asked Jesus when they saw the blind man in John 9: "Rabbi, who sinned, this man or his parents, that he was born blind?" (verse 2).

The disciples wanted an explanation. There had to be a definitive answer to the why of blindness. Isn't there a definite answer to the why of CP? Did Scottie do something? Did his parents? Who is at fault?

Jesus' answer was an unusual one: "Neither this man nor his parents sinned, but that the works of God should be revealed in him" (verse 3). I don't have a better answer myself. But even this inspired answer doesn't seem to be enough.

When I ponder handicaps where no one seems to be at fault, I often question God. I wrestle with the question, "Is God just?" The prophet Habakkuk wrestled with this same problem in the Old Testament. He looked at his world and saw atrocities and cried out to God, asking, "Why?" Habakkuk was upset with the injustices in the land of Judah where good things were happening to bad people and bad things were happening to good people.

When God answered Habakkuk, He merely stated it would get worse. Habakkuk was told that the Babylonians would destroy his people. The problem was that the Babylonians were worse than the people Habakkuk complained about. Evidently, Habakkuk believed in the inevitability of the bad news because his next question was about how long God was going to let the injustices continue.

God's answer is the closest thing we will find to an answer for the whys of life, but you may not like it. The difficulty is that God doesn't give a logical answer to the problem of human suffering. He merely states, "The righteous will live by his faith" (Habakkuk 2:4). It doesn't make sense. It is not the conclusion that we desire, but it is God's kind of answer.

Living by Faith

God's answer doesn't really tell us how the problem got there. But it does tell us how to exist in the midst of it. It's three words in the original Bible: righteousness, live, and faith. If we want to be right with God, if we want to truly live, then we must have faith in God. We may not understand it necessarily, but we do have what is most important: being right with God and finding true life.

The first friend with CP that I ever had was Duane Anderson. In fact, he introduced me to Scottie. Duane was a character. He couldn't talk as well as Scottie but loved to talk every chance he got. His favorite thing to do was to interrupt sermons with off-the-wall humor. Scottie imitated Duane's interruptions but never quite had the humor. If Duane was around, everybody knew it. He was the life of the party. Because of his great intellect and outstanding humor, it seemed so unfair

25

that he couldn't talk very well. And yet, I don't know anyone who influenced or entertained more people than Duane. He couldn't talk, but he could definitely communicate.

Duane decided to use his leadership ability to start an outreach to people with CP. And Duane didn't want to do anything in a small way. As a result, he brought so many people with CP to church that we had to acquire a special bus for transportation. When we had retreats, Duane wanted everybody with CP there. It may have caused transportation, lodging, and eating problems, but it didn't matter to Duane. He was on a mission to save anyone who had CP.

On one of these weekend retreats, a traveling preacher named Stanley Shipp was the resource person. During Stanley's sermon, someone in the audience noticed Duane's friend Ila Mae Morgan who also had CP and was confined to a wheelchair. Ila Mae is a story in and of herself. If you look carefully at her wheelchair, you will see a bumper sticker that says, "Attitudes are the only disability." Duane had brought her on the retreat to introduce her to his friends at church. But the presence of all these people with CP made one person very uneasy, so right in the middle of Stanley's talk, he interrupted with a question.

"Why is Ila Mae in that wheelchair?" he asked. It was

like the question asked of Jesus about the blind man. It was meant to stump Stanley or make God look bad. There was a hush in the crowd. Would Stanley attempt to field the question?

Without hesitation, Stanley looked the young man in the eyes and said, "So you can push her!"

Now that answer certainly doesn't explain everything, but it wasn't half bad. Because when you start pushing the Ila Maes of this world around, everything in your world begins to look differently. You begin to see the world through the eyes of Jesus. I call it joining the Order of the Towel.

The Order of the Towel

I first noticed the Order of the Towel in the events surrounding Bertha Bloss. I never knew how to explain her. It seemed as if she was always hanging around our house when I was growing up as a child. Mrs. Bloss wasn't my grandmother, or any relative for that matter. She didn't live nearby. She didn't go to our church. She was simply a poor, old lady who had ended up in my hometown because her son had been committed to a mental institution there.

And so my mother took care of her. She was with us on holidays. We brought groceries to her house. Frequently, we gave Mrs. Bloss and her mentally ill son rides in our car. I found myself often bringing presents to Mrs. Bloss, and even to her son. My mother pretty well took care of whatever they needed until they died.

And then something else strange happened after their deaths. Another old woman and then another just kept entering my mother's life. I didn't have an explanation for it as a child. But now, it makes sense to me: My mother many years ago entered the Order of the Towel.

The Order of the Towel was instituted in the Upper Room when Jesus washed the feet of His disciples in John 13. Here He showed the incredible servant nature of His love. But there is an interesting introduction to this passage in verse 1: "It was just before the Passover Feast. Jesus knew that the time had come for him to leave this world and go to the Father. Having loved his own who were in the world, he now showed them the full extent of his love."

In this act of service, John says that we see the "full extent" of Jesus' love. Now I would expect that statement to be in John 19. I would think that the "full extent of His love" was demonstrated at the cross rather than in the washing of feet. If John wasn't going to describe the death of Christ as the full extent of His love, then surely it would be an appropriate designation for His incarnation or resurrection.

But those are places where Jesus shows heroic service. Only Jesus could have been the God who became flesh. Only Jesus could have died for our sins. Only Jesus could conquer death for our salvation. But anyone could have washed feet. This shows the full extent of Jesus' love. He did what anyone could have done, but no one was doing. There was a need. Everyone saw it. Anyone could have done it. All ignored it. And Jesus humbled himself and did it.

Why did he do it? To start a new sacrament? No. There was simply a need—dirty feet—and no one seemed willing to do anything about it. You can read too much into this passage. What it boils down to is there was a need that anyone could have met. But only Jesus met it.

I asked, "Ila Mae, what does it mean to wash feet?"

She said, "It means taking care of somebody when no one expects you to and when no one will pay you back." She further told me she knew what it was like to have her feet washed because people have to do everything for her. Ila Mae said she knew how it felt to need something done and then watch everybody just looking around to see if someone else would take the initiative to do it. She added that there was one place where she most frequently found foot washing taking place, and that was at church. Ila Mae said, "I have a lot of people in my life who serve me, but it is not foot washing. They have to do it because the state pays them to do it. But at church, people do it because they want to do it."

Scottie-ism #2
Do what anyone can do, but no one is doing.

Anyone can push a wheelchair. Anyone can feed Ila Mae. There are seldom volunteers for bathroom duty even though everyone is qualified.

We are often so caught up in our giftedness (what only I can do) that we miss out on the full extent of love. It is doing what anyone can do, but no one is doing.

I loved Scottie because he gave me a chance to serve like Jesus. He needed me for all sorts of service. Anyone could have done it, but not many did. In the end, I don't know what Scottie would have done without me. I served him well. But he served me better by giving me an opportunity to "push" him.

Last Martin Luther King Jr. Day, I was playing his famous sermon "I've Been to the Mountaintop" to our children at the Northwest Church. Most of us are familiar with the famous parts of the speech where Dr. King talks about going to the mountaintop and seeing the other side. But many of us aren't familiar with his text and the points from it.

The text of the sermon was the parable of the Good Samaritan (Luke 10:30-37). And from his lesson, Dr. King helped me see the questions that mark not only the differences in the Good Samaritan and the priest and Levite, but also the differences between Jesus and His disciples in John 13.

King said that the question that the Levite and priest asked when they saw the needy man on the side of the road was, "What will happen to me if I help this person?" Walking by someone in need is not an aggressive evil. No, it is simply a sin of omission. The priest and Levite just don't get involved because it demands something of them. It requires a loss of time, money, position, pride, power, or it's a religious hassle because this person is not like us. We see a lot of this kind of evil don't we? "What will happen to me if I help this person?"

The Samaritan was called good because he finally asked the right question: "What will happen to him if I don't help?" And then he helps. Good is when you get your focus off yourself, see someone else's need, and do something about it. And this is exactly what is happening in John 13. The disciples are looking around wondering, "What will happen to me if I help?"

Jesus asked, "What will happen to them if I don't

help?" This is the essence of why Jesus came. What would happen to us if He didn't come? This is why He went to the cross right after the Upper Room. Because what will happen to us if He doesn't help?

And He tells us to do the same thing: "Now that I, your Lord and Teacher, have washed your feet, you also should wash one another's feet" (John 13:14).

What is going to happen to this world if we don't help? And what about the Scotties of this world? What will happen to them if we don't help?

Perhaps we are worried about what we might lose: our time, our pride, our money, and our convenience. And yet it is right here in this loss that we find what we have been looking for—life. Yes, Jesus tells us that when we lose our life, then we find it (Matthew 16:25).

I still can't answer all the whys of CP in any logical format, but when all is said and done, in helping Scottie—I found life.

Milton Jones

*M*ilton Jones. That's what Scottie's nametag usually said. Yes, he would put my name on his nametag. Now Scottie couldn't prepare his own nametag, but anytime he could talk someone into it, his nametag would say "Milton Jones."

That nametag created interesting conversations around the church. When people would meet Scottie for the first time, they couldn't understand his speech. So in order to get his name, they would have to read his nametag. Later when the person would meet me, he or she would say, "I thought he was Milton Jones." And even when we didn't wear nametags, Scottie was likely to introduce himself as Milton Jones.

Scottie liked my name. And he liked using my name. He tried to be like me. When he would go to Carol Hubbard for a haircut, he would always tell her to trim his hair so he would look just like Milton Jones. Now, that's funny because Scottie was one hairy man. He had thick, jet-black hair that wasn't very manageable. He looked as if he could use a haircut about every other day. My hair, on the other hand, is rather fine and brown. There's no way on earth he could get his hair to remotely resemble mine. But at the end of the haircut, Scottie would examine it and conclude that he looked just like Milton Jones.

If Scottie wasn't wearing my name, he was using it to his advantage. Anytime he found something that he didn't like, he would announce that he was going to tell Milton Jones. Yes, if there was any way to get one step ahead by using my name, Scottie would do it.

Why did Scottie do this? Was he a big liar? That would be too simple an answer. Was Scottie delusional? Did he really think he was me? Scottie had some mental challenges, but I don't think that's the answer either.

Why did Scottie use my name? The answer is simple. He liked me. He wanted to be like me. Life seemed to work better for me than it usually did for him. And so he simply tried living my life as best as he could.

From Scottie's viewpoint, my life was pretty exciting.

People paid attention to me. I went places. I had things that Scottie couldn't have because of his disabilities. So the closest he could get to a different life was assuming my identity.

Scottie, like all of us, wanted people to pay attention to him. And Scottie rarely got the time of day from most of them. People with CP easily become invisible. Because of their lack of ability to talk clearly, people often walk right past them as if they can't communicate at all. When Scottie became me, however, it was a different story. People paid attention. They laughed at the joke of wearing someone else's name. He was no longer Scottie. He was Scottie, Milt's friend. The conversation surrounding him would shift to topics that were more interesting than those in his ordinary life. I traveled. I preached. I wrote books. Scottie stayed home. Scottie listened. Scottie had CP.

Scottie took it so far that he got his parents to buy him a microphone so he could preach like me. He went into his room and preached my sermons. When he got a chance, he would stand behind the pulpit at church and pretend he was me. If someone called him on the joke, he would smile and argue with them. "I am Milton Jones," Scottie would say. When we were together, it was like the old television show *To Tell the Truth*. Three persons would all stand up and say, "My name is . . ." Then it was up to the panelists to figure out who the "real" person was. But in this case, everyone already knew it was me. Scottie knew that too, but he enjoyed it nonetheless.

When I would visit him at his group home, new workers were always interested in meeting me. They often thought that Milton Jones was some imaginary creature made up by Scottie. When I walked into the group home, they would give a sigh of relief that Scottie didn't have a six-foot invisible rabbit that he talked to. No, he had a real preacher.

But I had to ask myself whether I liked Scottie using my name. This was truly strange behavior. Did I mind? Not at all. I was kind of honored that Scottie liked me. I didn't mind him using my name because I liked him too. If anyone was going to use my name, I couldn't think of anyone better than Scottie.

There's an old story about a young thief in Napoleon's army. When he was arrested for petty thievery among the troops, his superior officer was going to execute him to make an example and deter further robbery. As he was being arrested, Napoleon intervened to ask about the situation. When Napoleon asked the lad his name, he answered, "Napoleon." He had been named after the great military leader. Moved by the boy's name being his own, the general pardoned him.

Several months later, the young man was caught stealing again. As he was being led away, he caught a glimpse of the general and cried out, "I'm Napoleon!" Once again the general talked to him and gave him another chance. Then Napoleon gave his parting words to the boy: "Either change your ways or change your name!"

If someone is going to wear your name, you want to know what kind of person he is. You don't want a scoundrel wearing your name. You value your name and don't want anyone to reflect negatively on your name. But Scottie—that's another deal. I was happy for him to wear my name just like he was.

Wearing Jesus' Name

I wear the name of Jesus. I call myself a Christian. It wasn't until I met Scottie that I ever thought about how Jesus might feel about me wearing His name. Why do I wear His name? I want to be like Him. More happens with His name than with mine. In fact, I use His name for my advantage anytime I can. His name is the only one that saves me. I call on His name when I'm in trouble. I call on His name when I have a need. I try to be like Him as much as I possibly can.

From His vantage point, I probably look pretty funny—like Scottie getting a haircut to be like me. But there are times when I look at myself and think that I'm looking like Jesus. Maybe to an outsider I don't look that much like Him, but to me, it's about as close as I can get at that moment.

I don't think Jesus minds my wearing His name. In fact, there is probably nothing He likes better. He is honored when I want to be like Him. He is happy when I use His name. And He gives me special privileges and a relationship with Him just because I do. In the past, I felt guilty wearing His name because there were so many parts of my life that didn't look like His life. I was ashamed because I was so inferior. My resemblance was simply not that close.

But Scottie helped me understand. I knew Scottie didn't look much like me or do things very similarly to me. But I loved him so much that I was totally honored that he tried. I wasn't upset that he didn't totally measure up to me. I simply felt warm every time I saw him trying to imitate me because of his love for me.

Doesn't Jesus feel the same way? He knows that we are not like Him in many ways. But don't you think He is honored every time we try to be like Him because of our love for Him?

So when I say I'm like Christ, I'm not lying or delusional. Deep down inside I know the difference (just like Scottie). And similarly to Scottie and me, I so much want to be like Jesus.

What Would Jesus Do?

Some years ago, I gave Scottie the book *In His Steps*. He always kept it near his bed. I gave it to him after a sermon that I preached one Sunday. After the sermon, I put a little sign on the pulpit. Scottie loved the sign. But he was so short that I would have to lift him up to see it. The sign was attached to the pulpit because of a good friend of Scottie's named Bill Roberts.

The little sign on the Northwest pulpit asks the striking question: "What Would Jesus Do?"

This sign was put on the pulpit in response to a sermon I preached many years ago. As I looked down the aisle during the invitation song, I could see Bill Roberts making his way to the front. As we sang, "Where He Leads Me, I Will Follow," I knew that some people would come. It had been a good sermon; the invitation had been a strong one. And Bill Roberts believed in making strong commitments.

My sermon had been based on Charles Sheldon's classic book, *In His Steps*. It's the story of a preacher, Henry Maxwell, who upon neglecting to help a down-and-outer who died, preached a sermon from the text of 1 Peter 2:21: "To this you were called, because Christ suffered for you, leaving you an example, that you should follow in his steps." At the conclusion of the sermon,

Maxwell invited the congregation to commit for a year to asking the question, "What would Jesus do?" before they made any decisions in their lives. And then they would try to do what Jesus would do, no matter what the cost.

I had decided to preach the same text and ask the congregation to make a similar commitment. If they were willing to ask, "What would Jesus do?" and do it, they were to write me a note or respond publicly to the invitation. And now here was Bill walking down the aisle.

The first time I met Bill Roberts was the first time in his life he had ever gone to church. A young woman from his office had invited him to attend our Sunday morning assembly. It was an eventful day for Bill. My sermon that day was on the second coming of Jesus. I preached that Jesus could come back at any minute, and then there would be a judgment. Bill believed what he heard, and it scared him to death.

The next morning Bill called me from work and told me that he wanted to be baptized. I asked him when he would like to do it. He said immediately because Jesus might come back very soon.

We met at the church building, and I proceeded to explain the gospel to him from the Bible. I'll never forget what happened when I opened up the Word. Bill said, "That's a first."

"What do you mean?" I asked.

He responded, "That's the first time I've ever looked at an open Bible."

I couldn't believe it. He was forty-one years old, living in Seattle, and had never read a word from the Bible. I continued telling him the story of Jesus and how we should respond to Him. I also explained the cost of following in the steps of Jesus.

After about two hours of studying the Bible, Bill said, "Milt, I promise that I'll read that book every day for the rest of my life. Now can I please be baptized? Jesus may be coming back at any minute!" Bill was baptized, and, as far as I know, he's kept that promise.

Now Bill was walking down the aisle in response to the question, "What would Jesus do?" I was ready for him to tell me, "Great sermon, Milt. It's about time you preached a hard-hitting message on discipleship."

Instead Bill said, "Milt, that's the most confusing sermon I've ever heard you preach."

Confusing? I don't know how I could have been more clear. I was asking the church members to figure out what Jesus would do and then do it no matter what the cost.

Then Bill continued. "Yes, Milt, it's the most confusing sermon I've heard here. Are you trying to tell me that I'm sitting here in the middle of a church that hasn't even decided if it wants to follow in the steps of Jesus? That's what you told me I was supposed to do when I became a Christian!"

Scottie's friend Bill reminded us of the decision that we should have already made. I have decided that I want to be like Jesus in every way that I can. I may fail. I may not look much like Him at times, but the goal is clear. I am to try to imitate Him and be like Him. I am to walk in His steps because I wear His name.

Follow Me

I learned the importance of being who I ought to be from Scottie. Scottie had decided whom he was going to follow. But, you might say, Scottie was following me. Scottie was smarter than that. He knew whom I was following. He was listening. He was paying attention. He knew exactly what Paul meant when he said, "Follow my example, as I follow the example of Christ" (1 Cor. 11:1). Scottie was following me as long as I was following Christ. He knew the difference, but he was looking for someone with a face to follow.

Scottie taught me an important reproduction principle: You reproduce after your own kind whether you like it or not. Certainly this is true biologically, but it is also true spiritually. You can tell people not to look at you but only at Christ. You can tell people not to follow you but only Christ. But the truth is that people close to you are going to imitate you whether you like it or not. So you'd better watch yourself.

Scottie-ism #3
Be the person you want others to be.

Edgar Guest put it well in the first verse of his famous poem "Sermons We See":

I'd rather see a sermon than hear one any day;
I'd rather one should walk with me than merely
    tell the way.
The eye's a better pupil and more willing
    than the ear,
Fine counsel is confusing, but example's
    always clear;
And best of all the preachers are the men
    who live their creeds,
For to see good put in action is what
    everybody needs.

Other people are watching you all the time, and they are imitating you whether you realize it or not. This is especially true with our children. They try to be like us in every way they can. They imitate our looks, habits, and speech. It's scary when they reproduce one of our own bad traits.

I train students to preach. I have an annoying habit of playing with my wedding ring and rolling it around on my finger when I preach. It is so habitual that I don't even notice it. I was listening to one of my past students preach the other day and noticed he was playing with his wedding ring throughout the whole sermon. He didn't mean to get that from me. But Scottie is another case when he preaches; his desire is to copy every idiosyncrasy that I have when I preach—like one of those impersonators. He wants to do it in such a way that someone will notice him and say, "You look just like Milton Jones!"

I think that is exactly what Jesus is looking for. For someone, someplace to stop and point at you and exclaim, "You look just like Jesus Christ!"

4
Pants

I've heard insecurity described as a man who wore both a belt and suspenders. If that's true, Scottie must have been very secure because he wore neither. And this created a problem. Upon numerous occasions, and most often in the church foyer, Scottie's pants fell down. We could never talk him into wearing a belt or suspenders. Because of the odd shape of his torso, pants never fit him very well. And because he always had to walk with both hands on his crutches, he never had a free hand to hold them up. As a result, when you heard the word, "Pants!" you were probably going to find Scottie's down around his ankles.

To have your pants fall down in public is pretty embarrassing. But so much of Scottie's life was. Scottie couldn't pull his own pants up. Someone had to do it for him. Scottie couldn't dress himself. He couldn't bathe himself. He usually needed help when he went to the restroom.

Scottie needed people. He couldn't make it alone; he was dependent on others for their help. He had to learn to operate on other people's schedules and he had to wait until the people around him decided it was time to help him.

Dependence can be pretty frustrating, but it can also develop some pretty important attributes, especially patience. When you have to learn to wait on people, maybe it is easier to wait on the Lord. When you have to be dependent on people, maybe it is easier to be dependent on God. Scottie was dependent on the Lord in the same way that he was dependent on everyone else in his life. I, on the other hand, struggle with independence. I start believing that I can really do things by myself. At times, I forget how much I need other people. And too often, I forget how much I need God.

Gift of Grace

Since Scottie was dependent on others, his resources and wealth were determined by what was given to him.

As a result, he was extremely grateful when anyone gave him anything. He seemed to understand the concept of grace better than most. He knew how to accept a gift. It was his only way to obtain most anything in his life. He was well aware that he could not make it and would not be alive for long if people didn't show mercy to him daily. He was not ashamed of this; it was simply the way he lived.

He didn't seem to think it necessary to earn acceptance with God. He readily acknowledged that God wanted to give him salvation. So Scottie was eager to accept the gift. Scottie knew that he could never earn or achieve for himself anything very big. And if salvation was the ultimate, then it was only natural for him to believe that it would be a gift, too.

Simple Contentment

When it came to lifestyle, Scottie also believed in grace. When you are dependent on others, it seems like you are more easily satisfied. Scottie was content with what he had. If you went into his room at the group home, you wouldn't find much; Scottie had few possessions. There weren't many clothes in the closet. He was thrilled that someone had given him a cassette tape player. He was thankful somebody was going to cook him a meal each night. Having his own room and bed was a really good deal in Scottie's eyes.

Scottie had a good grasp of what Paul told Timothy: "But if we have food and clothing, we will be content with that" (1 Tim. 6:8). The bottom line for contentment, according to Paul, was food and clothing. Scottie thought anything above these necessities was a bonus. Therefore, all he needed to be happy was food and clothing. When this became his standard, he found contentment. He had the basics, and he had the bonus too.

As simple as his life was, Scottie still had a lot more than food and clothing. He had a bed. He had cool, black leisure suits, not just clothes. He had music to listen to and even tapes of his favorite preacher. He had art to look at. He had all kinds of little things. A lifestyle that might have seemed like poverty to me was full of fringe benefits to Scottie.

Scottie taught me how materialistic I had become. He was satisfied and content with very little. Yet the more I accumulated, the more I seemed to want. He taught me that stuff doesn't bring happiness. When I looked in his room and saw how happy he was and how proud he was of what he had, I was convicted to live my life more simply.

Scottie got more thrilled with a new postcard than I do with a new car. In fact, Scottie started collecting beautiful pictures. He loved them. He never bought them. They were simply pictures that he could some-how acquire for free. Usually they were postcards given out at art exhibitions, but a beautiful picture from a magazine was also very appealing to Scottie. When you visited him, he would show you his pictures proudly, and then he would give you one. "Freely you have received, freely give" (Matthew 10:8).

Honest Confessions

Nancy Vinson, a caseworker helping Scottie in some art classes, took the time to talk to Scottie and write down his story. It's the only autobiography of him that exists. Let me share it with you. I think it is pretty accu-rate except for his age. I asked him about a million times, and he never once knew how old he was.

My name is Scott Callis. I am thirty-seven years old. I've had cerebral palsy all my life. Sometimes I talk a little funny. Please ask me to repeat myself. I don't mind. Please let me make my own decisions; it is very important to me. If I'm not part of the decisions to do with me, I probably won't do it. I've been to Artists Unlimit-ed before, and I am real excited to start up again. Sometimes I need things explained to me several times before I remember. Please be patient.

What is surprising about Scottie's autobiography is how up-front and honest he was with his limitations. After his age, he thought his most striking feature was his handicap. In reality, most people noticed his disability before his age. Instead of apologizing or being embarrassed, Scottie was simply honest. He knew who he was, and he accepted who he was along with his limitations.

And when it comes to understanding how to be gracious to him, Scottie is also very up-front. He tells you what he needs, and he doesn't ask for much. He doesn't ask for anything more than a little time and patience. He simply asks to be a part of his own life. He is dependent. He doesn't want independence, but he does appreciate a choice.

Isn't that exactly what God gives us? He just asks us to confess honestly who we are and admit our limitations. He wants us to make Him the Lord of our lives. That means that we become dependent rather than independent. But through it all, He still gives us the choice. That's faith.

Listen

The greatest kindness, in Scottie's view, was when you attempted to communicate with him. He knew that he would be difficult to understand. He knew that you would have to try over and over again to decipher his words. He just appreciated that you took the time to try.

Maybe that is how God feels, too. He knows that we may not completely understand His will or His words. But nothing pleases Him more than us taking some time to communicate with Him. Whether it is listening or talking, He seems to appreciate and love the effort. Time spent together trying to communicate appears to be more important than perfect communication.

Probably the saddest part of CP is the loneliness. I see it over and over again. It's not the loneliness of being alone. It is the loneliness that comes from being ignored. Time after time I've seen people walk right by a person with CP and say nothing. And people with CP have no trouble hearing. But not even a "hello" is usually offered. People treat them as if they can't hear.

Most people ignore people with CP because they are afraid that the person with CP might actually say something. And when they do speak, they are fearful that they probably won't understand it. And it would be embarrassing to ask them to repeat it. What if you had to ask them to repeat it over and over again?

But people with CP count it the greatest kindness to be listened to. They are smart. They know that they are hard to understand, and they don't mind repeating themselves nearly as badly as they hate being ignored.

This is so true that Scottie included it in the few sentences summarizing his life. The essence of grace to him was a person being patient enough to listen.

Mike Dahlager goes to the Northwest Church and also has CP. He sits in a wheelchair in the aisle every Sunday morning, Sunday evening, and any other time the doors are open. He can't talk as well as Scottie, but he communicates with a computerized message board where he spells out anything he wants to share. It is amazing to watch him type out his words. He is extremely immobile because of the stiffness in his arms, and yet he manages to get his message across.

Mike is one of the funniest men on earth. How tragic it is that so few know his funny side. Mike pays attention to every word of my sermons. At the end of each sermon, he comes up beside me and makes a hilarious comment. And each little remark spins directly off a point in my sermon. Mike lives to give me a hard time. Recently, I had been traveling for a few weeks preaching elsewhere. When I got back to church I said, "Hi, Mike!" He merely replied, "Who are you?" Within minutes he was introducing me to everyone as the visiting preacher.

Mike is a delight. But even at church among the best people I know, people walk right past him. Too often Mike is sitting in his wheelchair with no one talking to him. And all it would take to make Mike's day is to stop and give him the time to spell out a message. Mike knows people have difficulty communicating with people who have CP, so he goes to the extreme by trying not to be boring. His goal is to bring people a little joy and humor when they encounter him. Still, most people walk by. They simply aren't, as Scottie said, patient.

Most people in my life don't have CP. But too many are lonely. I received a call one day from a funeral home near Scottie's place. The funeral director asked me if I would do a funeral service for a lady. I quickly agreed. Then he said that it was going to be a bit unusual. I cringed. When people say "unusual" and "funeral" together, I get a little worried.

"What's going to be different?" I asked.

"No one is going to be there," he replied.

"What do you mean?"

He explained that they couldn't find anyone who knew her. But in her will she stated that she wanted someone from our church to do a funeral for her. She even left $300 for the occasion.

It was hard to write the sermon. I remembered the words to the old Beatles' tune:

Father McKenzie, writing the words of a sermon
    that no one would hear.
  No one comes near. . . .

53

All the lonely people
where do they all come from?
All the lonely people,
where do they all belong?"

As I stood there alone in the cemetery, preaching to no one, I wanted to shout out, "Doesn't anyone know this woman?" But I knew I wouldn't get an answer.

I don't want people to die alone. I don't want people to live alone either. Scottie talked to everyone he met. He didn't want anyone to get the same treatment he got. He figured if he always initiated conversation, he would be hard to avoid. When he got his job greeting people at Safeway, he was determined that no one would get by him without a greeting and a smile.

Talk!

One of the most tragic letters I've ever read was left on my desk when I was a campus minister at Texas Tech. It read:

VICTIM
I am a walking victim
That no one bothers to see
I am a walking victim
That no one bothers to hear

The streets shout their death

To the silent parking meters.

And I am left alone

I am a walking victim

That no one bothers to know

I am a walking victim

That no one wants to be

For in my face:

The greatest disease.

Loneliness this is me.

Scottie's autobiography was simply a cry not to be a walking victim. As he lived in the world of CP, he saw too many victims. He didn't want his life to be summarized by that one word, loneliness. And thank God it wasn't.

Loneliness can happen in the world of CP. It can happen anywhere. It can even happen at church. Another devastating letter I received went like this:

Hi—

I am a Christian.

I have been one for many years.

I exist.

I have a name.

I know you and I think

That you know me.

But you are so involved with

Your little group that you

Never speak to me.

I need your friendship . . .

I am a Christian.

But I am dying. . .

Love me—Talk!!

Signed . . .

The sad note ends with exactly what Scottie was asking for in life—"Love me—Talk!!"

Scottie-ism #4
If someone looks lonely, talk to them.

People need people. People need people to talk and listen to them. It's usually not what you say that makes a difference; it's that you care enough to say something. Scottie didn't have a degree in counseling, but he sure healed a lot of people by entering their world and giving them some words of kindness.

All of us want to be loved, but it is hard to feel loved if you are ignored. It is difficult to receive compassion in isolation. Scottie felt loved when people took the time to communicate with him.

Touch

In Mark 8 when Jesus touched the blind man, he didn't receive complete healing. He described his vision after the first touch as seeing "men as trees, walking" (verse 24, KJV). In order to have complete healing, he needed a second touch.

Many times in my life I have needed the second touch. I go around my world not noticing the people who walk by me. They might just as well be trees walking because I don't acknowledge them as real people whom God loves. I too often miss the people who are directly in front of me. When I go to one of those fast food places, it might as well be a Douglas fir tree waiting on me. I am too busy. I don't notice.

Scottie noticed. He listened. He looked. I often tell stories in my sermons of my travel disasters. I have flown near tornados, through Pacific storms, and lost my luggage on countless occasion. When people hear my stories, they usually die laughing. All except Scottie. He always yelled out, "Poor Milton!" He tried to see the events from my point of view. He really hated that I was inconvenienced and truly tried to feel my frustration. I wasn't just another tree walking for Scottie.

I've decided to ask Jesus for a second touch. I want to see people as people walking. I want to truly see them as Scottie always did. I want to notice them and acknowledge them. I want to love them and talk.

Machine 5

"Machine." Scottie nearly always said it before any assembly at our church. When he would leave he would usually say, "Machine?" as if maybe next time.

Now, an overhead projector was a "machine" to Scottie. Scottie liked overhead projectors. When Scottie first came to our congregation, we displayed all of the songs that we sang on overhead projectors. Scottie liked to sing, and he associated the joy that came from singing with overhead projectors. But Scottie became a victim of progress. Things changed.

One day our church quit using overhead projectors. Using a computer, we projected our songs onto a huge screen in the front of our auditorium. Scottie called this a "screen." Scottie didn't really like the screen. No, he wanted the machine. Scottie didn't like to change much. So every time we met, he said "machine" hoping it would be the day that we would go back to the way we were.

Scottie had preferences, and he wasn't interested in changing many of them. He liked to wear leisure suits. Yes, those old tacky ones that we hoped would disappear in the '70s. And he still wore those bright multicolored, big-collared rayon shirts underneath his leisure suit. One color dominated his wardrobe—black. Every suit he owned was black. If you went to his closet, all his clothes were the same. He had found what he liked. Why change? Fashion didn't dictate his own style. Scottie was one of a kind, and that was fine with him.

When it came to church, he sat in the same pew every week. For years, he sat in the pew directly in front of Bill and Lydia Gumerman. They moved, but Scottie didn't. Then John and Joann Smith moved to where the Gumermans sat. That change didn't bother Scottie because he got to stay the same.

Scottie liked the same preacher every week—me. If someone else came to preach, he would simply say, "No, Milton!" It could have been Billy Graham, and Scottie would have wanted me. He liked consistency in his world. He enjoyed keeping things the way they were.

Scottie liked the same food—pizza. He liked the same songs every week. He didn't ever want to move. He liked his room. Scottie had found what he was looking for so, why change?

There's something pretty special about finding what you are looking for. It produces happiness. Contentment breeds peacefulness, and that's good.

Go with the Flow

The problem occurs when you won't let others change because you don't want to change. Here is where Scottie shined. I never met anyone who wanted things to stay the same more than Scottie. But when things changed, he adapted. He expressed his opinion, and then went with the flow.

Every Sunday Scottie would say to me, "Machine!"

I would then reply, "No, Scottie, we are using the screen this week. It really gives us a better picture. Don't you think so?"

Then Scottie would sigh and tell the truth like he always did. "Yeah, but I like the machine."

But when the music started and the screen lit up, Scottie sang with all his heart. He sang zealously when watching a machine. He sang zealously when watching a screen. He could read words just as well off a screen as a machine, which was not at all.

Changes at our congregation were always challeng-
ing for Scottie. As our church got a little more contemporary in its worship style, Scottie didn't like it. He liked
the old ways. There were times when other people dis-
liked the changes so much that they left. Scottie was
also invited to leave on occasion. He didn't understand.
You express your opinion, according to Scottie, but you
don't have to have your way.

Scottie was sad when anyone left our congregation.
Scottie liked traditional worship better than anyone. But
Scottie was interested in worship itself more than the
form of it. The style may have changed, but God didn't
change for Scottie. He thought that God ought to be
praised, period. If we praised God his favorite way, he'd
do it. If we praised another way, he'd do it, too. He was
just glad to praise God.

Scottie had indeed found what most of us are looking for—contentment. Nothing had to change for Scottie
to be happy. He was happy with things the way they
were. Were things perfect in his life? Hardly, most things
were highly imperfect. If we were in Scottie's shoes, we
would have wanted our health to change in order to be
happy. We would need to be rid of CP to be content.
We would want a little more money, a better place to
live, convenient transportation, and a modern, up-to-
date wardrobe to be satisfied with our lives. But not

Scottie. In fact, he was the opposite of most of us. He enjoyed things just the way they were.

But change happens. When I was studying marketing in college, a professor told me that the only constant is change. I don't agree with his analysis, but the world certainly is changing a lot. Most of the technologies of the last decade bypassed Scottie. The Internet was way beyond his grasp. But he never demanded that people around him be like him. He just enjoyed his world and would accept your world even if it was different.

When Scottie and I couldn't make it to Godfather's Pizza, we would go to Burger King. It was the closest restaurant to the church building. We liked the old slogan there, "Have it your way." Scottie liked having things his way. He liked burgers his way. But he would eat it and not complain if they messed up the order and it wasn't his way.

Scottie-ism #5
Having it your way
is for burgers, not life.

Scottie loved being at church more than anything else in the world. He seemed to understand the truth that "Jesus Christ is the same yesterday and today and forever." (Heb. 13:8). If that is true, then why do things have to change at church? In fact, some of the things that Scottie loved most changed. We quit singing most of Scottie's favorite hymns and started singing new praise songs. We discontinued his favorite fellowship time between services where he could get coffee and donuts because our church had grown and the room was being used as a classroom. His favorite elder moved. We exchanged the big pulpit that Scottie loved for a little lectern. And worst of all, we started talking about moving the location of the church building.

Every single change was stressful for Scottie. But Scottie had learned to work through the stress caused by change.

Change is difficult and stressful for everyone. The more our world changes, the more difficult it becomes to cope with the changes. Chuck Swindoll described well the strains of stress: "Multiply one day's crises by 365. Add financial strain, inflation, traffic jams, unemployment, unplanned pregnancies, failure at school, obesity, smog, surgery, loneliness, alcoholism, drugs, and death. Subtract the support of the family unit. Divide by dozens of different opinions. . . and you come up with a formula that has the makings of madness. Block all avenues of escape and you have an enormous powder keg with a terribly short fuse. Even if you are a

Christian. . . and love God intensely. . . .and believe the Bible and genuinely want to walk in obedience."[2]

A doctor at the University of Washington where Scottie was sometimes treated for his medical difficulties did a study on change. He studied the major changes people go through in their lives. He then weighted each one of them with a number based upon how much that particular change caused stress in the average individual. He called these numbers "Life Change Units." What Dr. Holmes discovered was that if a person had a high number of LCUs (meaning a period when they experienced an extraordinary amount of change), they nearly always got sick. He concluded that a person should try to limit the number of changes in his life at any one time in order to stay healthy.

Scottie believed this. He didn't change much unless he had to. When an unwanted change was inevitable, Scottie would discuss his viewpoint with anyone who would listen to him. But when he saw that he was not going to get his way, he was not cantankerous and didn't grumble. Even if it wasn't his preference, Scottie accepted the new direction and tried to give it his all. In the end, Scottie learned to enjoy most of the changes in his life. He learned to like his new living situation. He loved his new job. And as he experienced worship in a different context, he found it to be highly uplifting.

Through the Circumstances

I've often heard the expression "Well, under the circumstances . . ." If Scottie had defined his life as "under the circumstances," he would have been extremely unhappy, because his circumstances were pretty rough. I heard a preacher one time say that Christians should live "above the circumstances." I liked that idea, but it wasn't very realistic. How could someone like Scottie live above the circumstances? He couldn't act as if the negative circumstances weren't there.

Scottie had learned to experience life like a ship in the ocean. If a ship is under the waves, it's going to sink. If it is above the waves, it is going to come down and crash hard. No, a ship has to be navigated through the waves. That's how Scottie navigated his life. He learned to travel with God's help "through the circumstances" and changes of his life. The changes and circumstances were always there. But he didn't let them get the best of him. No, he simply persevered through them.

My wife wrote a song for Scottie and some of his friends with CP. It was a favorite and gave Scottie some hope as he decided to strive on and navigate stormy waters.

Strive On

To serve like Jesus
Seems impossible to me
When so much of my own life
Depends on others serving me,
But I can serve a happy heart,
A listening ear, a smile
To someone who has none of these
And make their life worthwhile.

My life is filled with blessings,
Although it may seem poor,
I may not walk or talk too well,
But you can know for sure,
My Savior gives a blessing
Every minute, every day,
I have hope for tomorrow
And so I smile and say,

Strive on, keep on striving on,
Keep your eyes toward the Savior;
Keep striving on
Look up, look up, and see the Son,
He's shining for every one.

My body now is feeble,
My legs are bent and frail

But heaven holds a form for me

That's never going to fail,

I'll walk and talk with Jesus

For ever and a day,

So won't you come

And walk with me

So you can also say:

Strive on, keep on striving on,

Make your path the straight and narrow;

Keep striving on

It's tough, although the path, we know,

Is the path that leads us to the Lord.

–Barbie Jones

I Want You to Ask...

6

*L*ike Scottie himself, his sentences were short. Most of them consisted of a word or at most a few. All except the statement that he continually made to Steve Stroop.

Scottie truly respected Steve. Steve was a scientist with a Ph.D. from UCLA. Steve was always willing to give time, transportation, and talk to Scottie. Scottie knew he had something special with Steve. Scottie knew he was with someone smart—someone important. So for Steve, Scottie blurted out a big sentence:

"I want you to ask yourself a question—are you going to help your brother?"

At first inspection, this may seem like a selfish question. It sounded as if Scottie wanted something from Steve. But that wasn't the case. This was a global question. He was asking, "Are you going to do something important with your life?" He always wanted to make sure that we actually give ourselves to what should be a priority—helping people. Scottie was reminding Steve that he should make his life count. It was his way of saying, "Carpe diem!" I can assure you that those exact words never came out of Scottie's mouth, but Scottie seized the day in his own unique way.

Scottie didn't have a Ph.D. He wasn't a scientist. He spent most of his career bundling coat hangers. I didn't even know anyone did that. Maybe there is a machine somewhere that gathers coat hangers. But a few are still hand assembled by people like Scottie. It's not a very important job, or is it? It was important to Scottie. He was glad to have a job. It was his job. It was his contribution to the overall scheme of how everything fit together. People had to have coat hangers. People needed something to hang all their black polyester leisure suits on. Scottie did his part. He was changing the world one coat hanger at a time. Scottie was smart enough to know bundling coat hangers wasn't what Steve or I did. Scottie's job didn't look that important, but he didn't complain.

Later in his life, Scottie got a new job. He became a greeter at Safeway. Wow, was he excited about his new employment! And he took it seriously. He didn't want to miss a single person who walked into the store. Everyone deserved and everyone would receive a greeting. I'll never forget the day I went to see him at his new job. I got my greeting and then a scolding from Scottie, telling me that I couldn't hang around him and loiter (not his word) because he had a job to do. As much as he loved me and wanted to be with me, he had a job to do. And if it was his job, it would be done. No one was going to get into Safeway ungreeted.

Scottie was a short guy. But he was not a little person. He wanted his life to count. And I think it bothered him when he saw people with much greater resources than he had falling short of their potential. Scottie heeded the words of Solomon, "Whatever your hand finds to do, do it with all your might" (Ecclesiastes 9:10). Whether it was bundling coat hangers or doing nuclear research, Scottie thought you should give it your best.

The apostle Paul says, "Work hard and cheerfully at whatever you do, as though you were working for the Lord rather than for people" (Col. 3:23 NLT). In this passage, we learn that the goal of our labor is twofold—to work hard and to work happy. Scottie worked hard. No one was going to bundle coat hangers with greater diligence than Scottie. But the big difference in Scottie was not in his performance or efficiency. It was in his attitude. Scottie worked hard, but he mainly worked happy.

Fish Market Theology

Scottie liked taking trips. And he especially liked outings with me. One day a bunch of college students from Abilene, Texas, were visiting and helping the church. We decided to treat them by showing them downtown Seattle and taking them to the Pike Street Market. The market is possibly the most famous tourist attraction in Seattle. It is a farmer's market with all kinds of food, crafts, and street performers. But nothing at the market is more famous than the flying fish.

There are many places to buy fish at the market. But one store takes the fish business to new heights. It is Pike Place Fish. It is world famous because they throw fish. And I don't mean minnows. No, they hurl huge salmon all over the place. When you pick out a fish to buy, they start screaming fish codes at volumes that can be heard all over the market. Then they send your fish flying through the air to the counter. The fish is traveling at high speeds and soaring directly over people's heads. And the guy behind the counter never misses (much). It is an exciting event. And thousands gather to watch the spectacle every day. It is a gathering place filled with amusement and laughter. Scottie was with us on this trip, and no one was belly laughing harder than he was.

Pike Place Fish is not only a good spot to visit, it is also a world-famous place for teaching strategies for work environments. They have videos, books, and seminars to teach their philosophy of selling. They have four basic principles that govern how they do business.[3] You can ask anyone who works there, and they will gladly quote all four of these values as fast as you can blink an eye.

1. Make Their Day. They go to extremes to make your trip to the market memorable. How? They throw fish. They catch fish. They tell jokes. Recently, when I was at the market with the college students, the man behind the counter threw a huge salmon to another worker who was standing directly in front of me. It scared me to death. The fish was flying right at us. It was traveling at such a speed that I thought it would knock me out if it hit me. But the fish man in front of me caught it with skill and grace. He just turned around and smiled at me. What a catch! He was the Willie Mays of fish catching. Then the man behind the counter yelled at the man again. This time he was throwing an even bigger fish. Again it sailed to the man in front of me. This time I was relaxed. I knew he could catch a fish. But right when the fish got to him, he ducked. I had no time to put up my hands, and the huge fish whacked me right in the face.

There was a gasp at the market. No one could believe that I had been hit. But it didn't knock me out. In fact, when I came to my senses, it didn't even hurt. Then the laughter began. They had thrown a stuffed fish. It was like a pillow. The first one was real to set up the second that was a fake. Everyone fell for it. They had made everyone's day. I was a celebrity—the guy who took a fish in the face and lived to talk about it. I had quite a story for Sunday's sermon.

2. Play. A lot of people sell fish. Pike Place Fish decided to have a lot of fun when they sold fish. So they threw their fish. Working at this fish market was like going to an adult playground. Everyone was having a good time.

3. Be Present. They try to make themselves absolutely present when they are with their customers. They give you the time of day; they look you in the eyes. In fact, they devote their complete attention to you when you are with them. They talk to you. They listen. They learn your names. And the fish people try to be completely helpful whether you buy a fish or not. But pretty soon you want to buy a fish simply because such service is so rare. And who wouldn't want to see another fish fly?

4. Choose Your Attitude. All of these principles are based upon this foundational philosophy. Most people wouldn't want to spend ten hours a day around a bunch of smelly fish. And yet the people who work at this fish market act as if they have the best job in the world. Most fish salespeople don't have to pick up heavy fish and throw them around. But these guys act as if they are among the privileged few. They decided that they could choose their attitude every day before going to work. And they all chose to have a good attitude.

Scottie loved the fish market. We always had a good time there. He would have made a good worker there. He couldn't have thrown fish very far, and he certainly couldn't catch one. But he had the attitude down. In fact, he lived by all four fish values but none more than the attitude.

Scottie didn't throw fish. He bundled coat hangers. But he chose to have a good attitude about every single coat hanger he picked up. We often think that our circumstances or environments determine our joy or sorrow. It's easy to think that where we have lived, who we have known and events that have taken place have determined who we are. It's true that circumstances affect us, but ultimately we are determined not by outward circumstances, but by our inner choices.

Power to Choose

Based upon three years' experience in a German concentration camp during World War II, Viktor Frankl was a victim of some of the greatest atrocities the world has ever known. His book, *Man's Search for Meaning*, reminisces on the lessons he learned from this horrific time. Dr. Frankl discovered that people survived the internment not necessarily based on their health or good fortune. No, they survived based upon their purpose. If people had meaning in their lives, they were much more likely to make it through the tragedies than if they had no reason or person to live for.

Frankl realized how survival related to attitude and wrote:

> We who lived in concentration camps can remember the men who walked through the huts comforting others, giving away their last piece of bread. They may have been few in number, but they offer sufficient proof that everything can be taken from a man but one thing; the last of human freedoms—to choose one's attitude in any given set of circumstances, to choose one's own way.[4]

Scottie didn't live in a concentration camp, but he certainly was trapped in a body that didn't work very well.

His life was full of problems. He lived in a world jam-packed with physical and emotional pain. Yet, he was happy. He chose his attitude.

Scottie-ism #6
Choose your attitude.
It may be your only choice.

Scottie couldn't choose most things in his world. He couldn't choose his occupation. He didn't get to decide where he would live. He certainly didn't get a choice concerning his disabilities. But he did choose his attitude. It was the one choice that he always could make. No one could take that choice away from him. Indeed, it is the last of our human freedoms, so Scottie chose well.

Gratitude

In Luke 17 Jesus healed ten lepers. Only one came back to thank him. Jesus wondered where the other nine were. Ten had been healed of leprosy, but only one had his heart changed. He came to Jesus because he had an attitude of gratitude.

Scottie might have been considered a social leper with all of his disabilities. People often didn't treat him well; he was an outcast in some circles. And his disease caused deformities and pain. As lepers were defined and named by their disease, so was Scottie. But Scottie was grateful, though he was never even healed of his disease. Nevertheless, he came back to say thanks with all of his CP still intact. His heart had been healed.

Scottie was going to enjoy his life with CP. If he couldn't enjoy life with CP, he simply wasn't going to enjoy his life. Because life, for Scottie, was going to occur only with CP. So he made his choice.

Scottie believed that his life counted. If others discounted it, he didn't. He believed that he was important in God's eyes. So Scottie valued his life, too. He had a purpose. His purpose on occasion revolved around coat hangers. At times it was praising God in song. Other times it was encouraging a friend like me. He wanted to do something with his life. He wanted to help a brother. And he wanted to make sure everyone else knew and valued their purpose, too.

So every once in a while a big question came out of a little guy. "I want you to ask yourself a question—are you going to help your brother?"

Fall *7* Away

*N*ow I certainly don't want to make it appear as if Scottie was perfect. As Scottie had problems on the outside, he also had some on the inside. And if there was one thing that plagued Scottie's inner nature, it was worry.

Scottie didn't worry about everything, but he tended to worry about the same things over and over again. And the worry that popped up again and again had to do with falling away. In Scottie's unique way of summarizing major concepts with a few words, he simply stated, "Fall away."

Scottie didn't want to fall away. What did he mean by this? At first, I thought he was dealing with one of the heavy theological battles that church people have fought over for years. Can people fall away from the Lord? Can Christians lose their salvation? Should I give Scottie a history lesson in the various views of this controversial issue that leads to the pros and cons of Calvinism? I don't think so. Scottie would think that I had lost my mind to talk to him like that.

But grace is a hard thing to grasp for a simple mind or a scholar. I tried to explain that salvation wasn't just a saved/lost proposition based upon what you did or didn't do last. I expounded upon how we are saved by being in Jesus, not by our achievements. My goal was to teach him how we could be confident in our salvation.

As I probed this issue with Scottie, I began to see that maybe this wasn't as deep a theological problem as I was making it. He just said, "Fall away." He didn't say, "Fall away from God." This made me wonder if he meant that he was worried that he wasn't going to keep his commitment at church. Maybe he was concerned that he would quit coming to church. It always bothered Scottie when he saw people who had been going to church for years stop attending. Perhaps he was worried that he would be the next one to leave, and he didn't want to fall away. After all, these were his best friends. To lose these relationships was more than Scottie wanted to think about. Or was it that he was concerned that we would forget about him? Maybe we would simply quit picking him up to bring him to church.

But after listening more to Scottie, I realized that his problem was a lot more basic. Scottie had no desire to leave the Lord. He never had and never would. And Scottie never missed church either. He had no desire to leave this congregation. Although he did try out another church for a short time, he certainly didn't want to go back there. And we weren't going to quit bringing him to church, though Scottie already had another way to get to church with mass transit. No, he wasn't even dependent on us for his transportation any longer.

Certainly leaving the Lord or church may have been plaguing his mind, but that wasn't his real issue. Those things weren't going to happen. Scottie simply had a worry problem. He let his mind think about bad things that hadn't happened or weren't going to happen. Scottie had a lot of time to think, and often the wrong things got stuck in that brain of his. And maybe you find yourself a whole lot like Scottie.

Let me tell you about two little sentences. They come from a story. Scottie liked stories. He couldn't tell them well because it was difficult for him to talk for any length of time without someone asking him to repeat himself. That's why he summarized big concepts with just a single word or at most a few.

But on the other hand, he loved to listen to stories. And he loved my stories. And if you listened well and knew what he was saying, he would tell my stories with a few words. It was like he would title my stories. Then he would say the title and hope everyone would remember the story connected with it. So this is "The Worry Story."

The Worry Story

During my freshmen year in college, I was worried to death. The Vietnam War was flourishing. And our government had started a lottery to decide who was going to serve in the military. I had problems with the war, and I didn't want to go. But I wasn't a draft dodger, so I mainly worried about it.

Lottery day finally came. I was sitting by myself at a table in the college student center consumed with my anxiety over the draft. From another room I heard some music playing, so I switched rooms to find out the source of the music. Again I sat alone and listened to this peculiar (at least for our campus) singing group. They called themselves The Horizons, and they were singing all about faith, hope, and Jesus. How they got to sing on this state campus I'll never know, but I allowed them to be the background music to my pity party.

A strange event happened in the middle of one of their songs. Right in the second verse of one of their gospel tunes, the tenor walked off stage, came down to my table and sat down. Maybe he was very perceptive or perhaps it was my face, but he said, "What's bugging you?"

I told him all about my anxieties and especially the draft deal. I couldn't believe that I was spilling my guts to a stranger. Then he gave me a Bible, a *Good News for Modern Man* version. I had never looked at a Bible that wasn't a King James before. As I glanced at it, I was impressed with its cool look and easy readability. He told me to keep it, but he also asked me if I would read a verse out loud. He wanted me to read Philippians 4:6-7.

In this new translation I read, "Don't worry about anything. Ask God for what you need. Always asking with a thankful heart. And God's peace which is far beyond human understanding will keep your hearts and minds safe in Christ Jesus our Lord."

The timely tenor then told me that this verse could be summarized in two sentences: Don't worry. Do pray. He explained that the reason I had so many worries was because I thought about the bad things that could happen in my life more than I prayed. He told me that most of the things I worry about will not happen, and if they do happen, they won't be as bad as my imagination or worry makes them. He went on to say that if I would pray every time a worry started to consume me, I would get what God promised me in this verse— peace. God's alternative to being stressed out, he explained, was a peace that was beyond our ability to understand. So we prayed about my worries (right there in the middle of the student center). It felt pretty good.

Then he gave me a pen and told me to write something in my Bible. I had never written in a Bible before—I didn't think you were supposed to do things like that. He told me to write the word draft beside this verse and date it. Then he told me that he hoped I would come back to that very Bible years from now and see that God had indeed taken care of me. And he hoped I would be even more convinced that His Word was true, and that my faith would have grown because I had learned to trust in Him. And he said I would believe more on that day than on this one.

Well, I left The Horizons to go listen to the radio and find out my number. Each birthday was given a number ranging from 1 to 365. Mine was 309. The government started with 1, so there was no way I was going to be drafted. God answered my prayer! But years later as I looked back, I remembered the student sitting beside me–his number was 6. He enlisted and went to

Vietnam. But God took care of him, too. In fact, he found the Lord while he was in the military. What I learned was that God was going to take care of me, no matter what. I learned that when I quit worrying and started praying. It was a matter of dependence on God rather than getting what you wanted that gave you peace.

Years ago, I quit using that *Good News for Modern Man* version. I had graduated to a New American Standard Bible and then to a New International Version. But one day I saw it on my shelf and picked it up. It was September 11, 2001. The academic dean where I teach told me that I needed to give a chapel talk. What would I say? I knew it was right there in that Bible. I opened that Bible and looked at a page that I hadn't seen in decades. Leaping off the page was a word— draft. And I thought about what had happened in my life over the last thirty years. At that moment, I realized that God had been faithful to me, and His Word had been true. And I believed more at that moment than I had on the day that I had been given that Bible. Now I knew what to say.

When I spoke to the students at the Christian college where I teach, indeed, they were worried, so I told them my worry story. In fact, I brought that old *Good News Bible* with me. I showed them where I had written the word draft. Then I asked them to write 9-11 in their Bibles. Next, I told them two sentences: Don't worry. Do Pray. I then said that I hoped that they would look at 9-11 in their Bibles years from now and see how God had been faithful to them. And they would find that God's Word had been true. And hopefully they would believe more on that day than they did on this day.

Do Pray

That's "The "Worry Story." Scottie couldn't tell the story, but he put it in his heart. And he could remember the two sentences: Don't worry. Do pray. And that's our next Scottie-ism because he must have said it a million times.

Scottie-ism #7
Don't worry. Do pray.

I told Scottie these two sentences every time he started worrying about falling away. He simply was to pray to God about the concern of his heart and his head.

I can think of a hundred times after the first telling of that story where Scottie would once again come up to me and say, "Fall away." I'd just say "Scottie, what are you supposed to remember?"

"Oh, yeah. Don't worry. Do pray."

I even wrote it down in his Bible. He couldn't read, but I think he knew what it meant. And he cherished the words that I had written there.

I don't think Scottie ever stopped worrying, but he never stopped praying either. And Scottie did find peace; and it was beyond comprehension and understanding. He may have had more peace than anyone I have ever known.

Scottie had more things to worry about on a physical level than I do, but it seemed that he had fewer things to worry about on the whole because his life was so less complicated than mine. I'm not sure who needed the lesson more. And my life is better to this day and every day when I remember those two little sentences.

"Fall away." That's probably not the source of your biggest worry. What do you worry about? We live in an age of worriers. We even worry that we worry too much. We seek all kinds of solutions, from alcohol to prescription drugs. But Scottie would assure you that nothing works better than prayer. It seems too simple. But in the end, it is doubtless the only thing that will work.

Notes

Scottie took notes on every word that I said from the pulpit. Scottie spent hours every day examining the pages of his Bible. Scottie could neither read nor write.

When I asked people what they remembered about Scottie, more people recalled his notes than anything else. If you were sitting in church listening to the preaching and glanced Scottie's way, you would see him writing with such an intensity that you thought it was a matter of life and death. Everyone would be impressed and comment on it.

Then one day you would happen to see the endless circles. At first glance, you would nearly die laughing. It was comical. There were reams of paper with circles on them. Then you would see that Scottie wasn't laughing. He laughed about nearly everything under the sun, but not his notes. It was serious business.

Why did Scottie take notes? I told everyone in the congregation that if they would take notes on my sermons, they would remember the spiritual lessons better. Scottie wanted to remember every word of my sermons, so he took notes. He couldn't write. He didn't have a clue how to even mark the alphabet on a piece of paper. But there was always a pen in his hand, and he always had a notebook with plenty of blank paper. When I started talking, he started writing. When I quit, he quit.

Scottie's writing was more cursive than block letters. But to be honest, his writing was simply a bunch of circles. It was like he was connecting endless loops of the lower case "e." It was amusing if you didn't know better. At first, we all chuckled when we saw that it didn't really spell anything. But Scottie read his notes. And Scottie remembered. So I always checked his notes after church and told him that they were very good.

One day Kent Landrum, one of my co-ministers at Northwest, was visiting Scottie in his room. He noticed a huge pile of spiral notebooks in a corner. He asked Scottie about them. Scottie told him that they were his notes from sermons. Kent looked at them, and every page looked exactly alike (just a bunch of circles with an occasional "S" and "T"). But the scary thing was when Scottie began to read them; they were actually different sermons to him. Could he actually read his own writing? Was it a code that only meant something to him? But the reality was that Scottie took notes and remembered the sermons from his notes.

Scottie read his Bible every day. At least he looked at nearly every page. Scottie wore out a good leather Bible every year, so it always made a good birthday present. I didn't have to think about what to buy Scottie; a new Bible would always make him happy. But he wanted a New International Version (that's what I use), and he wanted it black (that's Scottie's color). And he would tell you if you made a mistake on either.

Get to Know God

Why did Scottie spend time in the Bible turning its pages over and over again when he couldn't read? I told everyone in the congregation that if they would have a quiet time and read their Bible every day, they would know God better. Scottie believed me, so he looked at his Bible every day. He tried to wear it out. He couldn't read, but somehow he did get to know God better.

Here's what bothers me. Scottie took notes on every word of my sermons, and he couldn't write. Most of the people at church don't take notes, and they can write perfectly. Scottie studied his Bible every day, and he couldn't read. Most people at church don't have a daily quiet time, and they can read extraordinarily well.

Amen Attitude

Scottie had discipline. He wanted to do church right; he wanted to work hard at his faith.

One day I was talking jokingly about having an "amen corner." Scottie asked me what that was all about. I told him that they were the people who would "amen" at all the appropriate times in my sermon. I explained that they would sit on the front pews on the left side and be my vocal encouragement. As a result, Scottie started sitting in that section of the church every week. He never changed pews. He was going to be my "amen corner." He amened every chance he got. If there was ever a pause in the sermon, you could count on an amen from Scottie. He didn't quite grasp the appropriate times, but he tried. One time I asked one of those rhetorical questions where the obvious answer was negative (at least the obvious answer to everyone but Scottie). "Are we supposed to cheat on our income taxes?" Of course, Scottie shouted, "Amen!"

But Scottie was just trying to be more committed. He took Hebrews 10:25 seriously. He didn't want to "forsake the assembly as is the habit of some." If the doors were open, he was there. He was there for every assembly. He wanted to be in Sunday school. He was there for every special meeting. In other words, you could count on Scottie. It wasn't easy for Scottie to get to church. He had to start getting ready hours before he could go to any event. It took time for Scottie to dress, eat, and take his medicine. He had to arrange rides. When public transportation started giving him rides, they would only give him a general time for pickup. He had to be prepared two hours earlier than what should have been the designated time.

Privileged to Give

Scottie believed in tithing. He didn't have much money. He got a little from the government, he got a little more from his parents, and he got some from his job. Add it all together, and it wasn't very much. But he always gave. Anyone else in Scottie's position could have rationalized out of giving. He was poor. He needed the money. He didn't have enough. Not Scottie. He never missed an opportunity to give.

Some might think that the church was insensitive to take his tithe. Shouldn't Scottie be on the receiving end?

He hardly had any money. Scottie didn't see it that way. Scottie tithed. It was his privilege. It was his honor. If he was going to be out of town visiting his parents, he would let us know. He didn't want the church budget to be messed up simply because he was going to miss a Sunday. And he would try to make up his missed tithe when he got back.

If we had a special contribution for missions or needy children, Scottie was thrilled to give. He reminded me of the Philippians who gave out of their poverty because they had first given themselves. "For I testify that they gave as much as they were able, and even beyond their ability. Entirely on their own, they urgently pleaded with us for the privilege of sharing in this service to the saints. And they did not do as we expected, but they gave themselves first to the Lord and then to us in keeping with God's will" (2 Cor. 8:3-5).

The Difficult Path

Scottie wanted to join our church's men's ministry. It was called Sons of Shamgar. Mike Vantine, our men's ministry leader, thought it would be cool to name the ministry after an obscure biblical character, thus Shamgar. Only one verse mentions him: "After Ehud came Shamgar son of Anath, who struck down six hundred Philistines with an oxgoad. He too saved Israel" (Judges 3:31).

Mike thought that the men of the congregation should have a rite of passage into the ministry that would make them like Shamgar. As a result, all of the men who wanted to be Sons of Shamgar would be required to go through a boot camp with two physically demanding initiation rituals. The first involved a javelin, the nearest thing we could think of to represent Shamgar's oxgoad. Certainly, there is the possibility that Shamgar bopped the Philistines over the head with his oxgoad, but we took the higher interpretation and decided that he threw it. Fred Luke, who threw the javelin in the Munich Olympics, lives in our area and agreed to teach all of our men how to throw the javelin. We couldn't believe how hard it is to throw a javelin properly. It took all of our effort and strength.

And then we looked at Scottie. We offered him an excuse, "You don't have to do this, Scottie. It will be okay."

The javelin was twice as long as he was tall. He couldn't hold it and stay standing on his crutches. He didn't have the strength to throw it. But Scottie would have nothing to do with exemptions. He didn't want to be an honorary Son of Shamgar. He wanted to do the real thing. He listened to Fred's instruction and then hurled the javelin with all of his might. Somehow, he kept from falling on his face. And when that javelin landed a few feet in front of him, a thunderous applause came from every Son of Shamgar. It was as if Scottie had won the gold medal in the Olympics. Scottie smiled. Scottie laughed. He knew the length of the throw. He just didn't want to do things the easy way. He didn't want to opt out of anything simply because it was difficult or took a lot of effort.

But the next Shamgar task was even more difficult. Shamgar killed 600 Philistines. In our city we had recently been having some drive-by shootings. We decided that instead of drive-by shootings, Sons of Shamgar should have walk-by prayings. As a result, every Son of Shamgar was to walk past 600 homes and pray over them. It took a lot of effort for Scottie to walk a few feet. There was no way he could walk down the streets past 600 houses. But he did. We gave him the option of not doing it. We told him that he could still be a Son of Shamgar without the long journey. We tried to be as gracious as we knew how to be. We offered him a wheelchair, but he refused. He would walk. No matter how long it took him. No matter how many blisters he would get. No matter how tired he would become, Scottie was going to walk.

When Scottie was baptized years earlier, he wanted his baptism to be just like everyone else's. We baptize by immersion at our church. The steps were steep into our baptistry, and Scottie couldn't use his crutches. When he got into the water, it was nearly up to his ears. It took several people to hold him up then put him under the water. Scottie could have changed his view of how baptisms should be done, but he didn't. He had already discovered that most good things in life are difficult.

We try to encourage every single member in our congregation to be in a small group and have a ministry. Certainly, Scottie could have considered this to be the plan for the people without handicaps, but he fully participated in small groups. He never missed. And when it came to ministry, he chose the future facility ministry. Yes, Scottie wanted to be a part of the group who would design our new church building.

He worked a little every day drawing up plans. His building plans were more intricate than his notes, but you can imagine the final product, can't you? He would then turn in his plans and sit down with the architects to discuss the future of the church building. The committee would look at Scottie's drawings that looked more like an art project in an elementary school than a diagram for building construction, but I never heard a single person laugh. Scottie was thanked. Each and every one knew that he had put as much effort into his plans as the architect had into his detailed sketches.

Never Retreat

Scottie was disciplined. He would take the difficult road. He had done so all of his life. Can you imagine how difficult it was for him to learn to walk? When nearly everyone else with his handicap opted for the wheelchair, Scottie wanted to walk. His little legs couldn't hold him up or balance him either, so walking was nearly totally dependent on his upper-body strength. It was truly an amazing feat of strength, balance, and endurance. But he had to fall on his face time after time to learn this skill. When most others would have given up and had the best excuse in the world to quit, Scottie didn't. He persevered.

And talking was even more complex than walking. He couldn't pronounce the words properly. Speaking came with extreme difficulty. He had to try and try again even to get a sound that remotely resembled the word he was trying to say. When it was all said and done, with all of this effort, he knew good and well that most people would never take the time to listen to him. But he practiced and practiced until he could communicate words that could be distinguished by people like me. He could have opted for mechanical communication. But Scottie was going to go the path of greatest resistance. There would never be an easy way for Scottie.

As I stated, Scottie never missed church. You could count on one hand the times he was absent. Did Scottie get sick? Yes. Did he often feel bad? He felt bad most of the time. He just didn't tell anyone. But he was not going to let how he felt eliminate what was most important from his life. Scottie came to church when he was having heart attacks. He didn't know that they were heart attacks, but he certainly was experiencing pain. He chose to live above how he felt.

No Excuses

I have seen many people retreat and quit over the slightest inconveniences. People don't attend church for the smallest of excuses. A minor financial setback occurs, and there goes the tithe. New Year's resolutions for quiet times are gone by February. Not feeling well becomes an out for just about anything you don't want to do. Scottie had more good excuses for inactivity than anyone I know. He just didn't use them.

People have told me that if you do spiritual disciplines when you don't feel like it, then it is hypocrisy. Scottie would disagree. He would call it obedience. He always tried to find the best thing to do and then he did it whether he felt like it or not. He had to, because if he waited until he felt like it, it wouldn't happen at all. Scottie always had ailments. Everything was always going to be a struggle. He could either live by excuses or do what was best no matter how hard it was.

Scottie-ism #8
If you wait until you feel like
doing something difficult,
your wait will be very long.

Scottie simply didn't live by his feelings. His faith demanded obedience. Obedience demanded perseverance and pain, but Scottie thought it was worth it. He didn't complain after giving his last dollar. He didn't say he was tired after praying over his six-hundredth house. He didn't scold you for not listening more carefully after he had to repeat himself for the fourteenth time.

Scottie knew that if he waited until he felt like doing things that he wouldn't enter into the realm of faith very often. Scottie continually launched out into all kinds of spiritual activities that seemed impossible for him to do, but he did them anyway.

Scottie and I discussed an analogy of faith illustrated by a man who was standing on the edge of a cliff trying to jump. The leap represented the response to the call of God. The man decided that when he had enough faith, he would jump. But he just kept standing there. He never got enough faith to jump while he remained on the edge of the cliff. He only received faith when he jumped.

Perhaps it was a difficult analogy for the likes of Scottie, but he was a little bit deeper in this particular area than most of the rest of us.

Faith comes in the process. God gives the faith when you jump. If you wait until you feel like jumping, you will probably remain there for a long time. If you wait until you have an amazing belief system before you act upon what you should be doing, you will be standing there for a great while. God will give you the faith when you trust Him and throw yourself in His arms.

Over and over again those of us without Scottie's handicaps have found excuses. When I get more faith, I'll do it. Scottie would tell us to do it now.

Instead of feeling himself into acting, Scottie would act his way into feeling. After giving, going to church, taking notes, perusing his Bible, prayer walking, and all the other disciplines of his life, Scottie would always feel better. The spiritual uplift from obedience was always found to be greater than any physical or emotional drain that got in his way in the process.

Scottie usually didn't move very quickly. But if need

be he could hurry. If it were important or urgent enough, Scottie's eyes would bug out, and he would work his crutches with fury. I called it "Scottie on a mission." Scottie gave it his all and then some.

Paul told Timothy to "discipline yourself for the purpose of godliness" (1 Tim. 4:7, NASB). The word for discipline is tied to the concept of the gymnasium. He is telling us to work up a sweat when it comes to our faith. Many of us haven't worked up much perspiration when it comes to our faith. We have taken the easy way out. Scottie thought the easy way never paid off much. He always took the hard road. He took the way of the cross.

9
Calvary

*I*t was Scottie's favorite song: "At Calvary." Scottie simply called it "Calvary." He could never sing it enough.

Scottie especially loved it when Bill Lawrence would lead worship at our church. There was always a little hidden hope for Scottie that he might be called to the stage. Upon occasion, Bill would not only lead "At Calvary," but he would also call Scottie to the stage to direct it. I wish you could have seen his face light up as he rose from his pew. He would grab his crutches and then maneuver up the stairs of the stage. And somehow along the way, he would grab a hymnal. I really don't know how he did it. How could you climb the stairs on crutches carrying a hymnal? No problem for Scottie.

Scottie would then do an even better balancing act. He would lean on his crutches with his underarms. With his left hand, he would hold up the hymnal. Then with his right hand, he would wave and direct the congregation in singing. How he remained standing, I'll never know.

Now there were two things that were funny about the whole process. First, the hymnal. We don't use hymnals at Northwest. At least we haven't in years. But somehow Scottie always managed to have one. But that's not the humorous thing about the hymnal. Scottie always had his hymnal upside down. I don't know how he managed it. He couldn't read, but he could manage to get the hymnal upside down every single time. He never got it right. And when people would look up, they would see the upside down songbook. Most didn't know that Scottie couldn't read. You just couldn't keep from laughing.

The other funny thing was Bill Lawrence. Bill stood directly behind Scottie. When it was time for the song to begin, Bill would sing the instant Scottie began. And then Bill would be right behind and directly above Scottie waving his arm too. Bill really set the pitch and directed the timing of the song. But in all the times we sang it, Scottie never turned around. He never knew.

Scottie's face beamed when he led singing. His Cheshire cat grin somehow became angelic. An eerie visible gleam came out of his eyes. You could notice his eyes glowing even if you were on the back row of the building.

Pardon Multiplied

I'm not sure that Scottie could totally relate to the words of the song: "Years I spent in vanity and pride, caring not my Lord was crucified." Those words certainly didn't apply much to Scottie. Vanity and pride weren't high on the problem list of Scott Callis.

No, I think it is the chorus that caught Scottie's heart: "Mercy there was great and grace was free, pardon there was multiplied to me." Scottie lived in a world dependent on mercy and grace. Nearly everything in his life hinged upon someone's mercy and grace. He could do very little for himself. He knew that he couldn't make it through a single day unless people showed him mercy and grace by helping him do things he couldn't do for himself.

Scottie had to live with pardon. When he walked through a room, things would get bumped and fall over because of the way he walked. "Pardon me" was often his mantra. When he simply couldn't get the words he was saying into some pattern that you could understand, he would apologize for it—like it was his fault. Scottie acted as if he was inconveniencing people simply because he was disabled. But he learned this because of the way so many people treat the handicapped. As a result, he kept asking people to excuse him. So his favorite song talked of pardon being multiplied. Nothing was better than that in Scottie's world. To know that your mistakes would be excused over and over again was too good to be true.

Sing for the Lord

To put it simply, Scottie loved to worship. He couldn't sing very well, but he could sing loudly. No one made more of a joyful noise than Scottie. He was uninhibited; his volume was full blast. He sang at the top of his lungs. You could hear him above everyone else in the congregation. It didn't matter how off pitch he was, Scottie wasn't going to quiet down. He was singing for the Lord, not people.

Our church is known for its congregational singing. One day we decided to have an entire evening of singing and bring in a professional technician to record the event. Then we could make CDs of the event and sell them to all the people who wanted to hear our church sing. There was only one problem. Scottie showed up. When you sing at Northwest, you simply learn to sing around Scottie. His voice is always there, but you learn to ignore it when it comes to making harmony. But this recording got it all; you couldn't filter Scottie out. Anyone who would hear the recording and didn't know who it was would think that we were horrific. How could anyone tolerate a voice that loud and that off pitch? You just had to be there.

The bigger the crowd the better with Scottie. He loved big events; he called them "seminars." It didn't matter if it was a retreat, an evangelistic meeting, or an actual seminar—he called them all "seminars." He especially loved retreats. On most of our retreats, we would sing for hours on Saturday night. He would call out "Calvary" over and over again until we sang it. He figured if we were going to sing for two hours, he could get in at least one request.

Praise with Abandon

Scottie worshiped with abandon. He reminded me of David bringing the ark back to Israel and dancing before the Lord. Michal, David's wife, didn't appreciate David's lack of discretion in his worship. She looked down on him for going too far in his praise of God. I think there are a lot of Michals around today. When someone really goes for it in worship and praises God with abandon, the Michals of today still look down on them. They act like they are too strange, too emotional, or too charismatic.

But it was a little different with Scottie. He worshiped with all of his being and people cut him some slack. They would say, "That's just Scottie." It was as if handicapped people are excused from acting "normal" (reserved in worship). Many acted as if it was only Scottie's low IQ that caused him to be so unreserved.

My religious background was pretty unemotional. We didn't get into worship like Scottie. Praise was like a foreign country to us. We didn't raise hands or shout to the Lord. We acted as if that was for other church groups or other personalities. We focused on the intellect and sought a rational faith. No one was like Scottie. We would have tolerated Scottie because he had CP and couldn't be expected to behave like the rest of us. If he were like the rest of us, then he would have to tone it down too.

But I want to admit something to you. When I looked over at Scottie praising God, I didn't think he was giving it his all because he was mentally slow. As I watched him raising his hands (an accident waiting to happen with Scottie), clapping to the Lord (the hands hardly ever met each other) and singing with shouts (way off pitch) to the heavens, I became a little envious. He had something that I needed. Something that I desperately wanted. When it came to worship, it wasn't that he was different–it's that he was correct. We are supposed to give God all our heart, mind, soul, and strength.

Audience of One

When I worship, I look around at people. If I were to sing at the top of my lungs, I would be wondering what everyone else around me was thinking. The first time I ever raised my hands, I looked around to see if anyone was watching. My volume and demeanor tend to get regulated by what the people around me want and expect. And it isn't simply the people around me I'm thinking of. Too often I've got myself on my mind.

Scottie was thinking of God. He could care less what the rest of us were thinking when he was praising God. If we had asked him to sing softer, he would have turned the volume up. He simply wasn't singing for us. He didn't have a problem with his self-esteem when he was praising God. He wasn't worshiping for me or for himself. Worship was for God.

Scottie-ism #9
When you worship, God is
the audience.

Scottie realized that worship to God was first of all a vertical response. Certainly, we praise God corporately, but God sets the parameters, not people.

The apostle Paul asks, "Am I now trying to win the approval of men, or of God? Or am I trying to please men? If I were still trying to please men, I would not be a servant of Christ" (Gal. 1:10).

Scottie had made his choice. He was going to please God not men. I find that very difficult. My motives often get mixed. As a preacher, I care a lot about how others see me; I want people's approval. But Scottie got it right.

Something unusual happened with me, and I think it happened with most of the people at our congregation. We changed. We became more like Scottie. He was never going to become more like us when it came to worship. The expressions and heart of worship that Scottie displayed became more of the standard in our fellowship. It was like breaking through a barrier. Breaking out of our traditional styles and mechanics to an unleashed melody of praise became a reality.

Many times I turn around out of habit to see if Scottie is there. I want to see him worship. I want to watch him praise. But he is not there. And then I remember: I'm not supposed to be looking for people. I'm supposed to be looking for God. And He is still there.

Seeing God

I can't ever remember Scottie saying a bad word. He never told me a dirty joke–or anything crude for that matter. Inappropriate sexual talk never came out of his mouth. Sexual sin wasn't his biggest struggle.

Lust never seemed to captivate Scottie much. The things and people we look at in order to entice our sexual desires weren't what excited Scottie. He seemed to like looking elsewhere.

Sexual temptation is hard to deal with; it has to be one of our greatest struggles. Most people never seem to be able to say no to the lusts of life. From our lack of confession, it may seem that it's not a big dilemma. But most of us would be pretty ashamed if someone knew our private fantasies.

Perhaps we have wrongly approached the problem of lust. We tell others and ourselves just to stop it. Don't look. Don't go there. Stop doing that. And we try and try and try. We do our best to stop looking. And then we look again. We say we'll never go to that place or enter that site again. And then the next thing you know, we're there again. We say that this is the very last time we're going to do this. And then we're doing it one more time the very next day.

Putting off lustful thoughts and habits may not be the key to purity. Certainly it is necessary, but maybe it is not a strong enough motivation to change our mind-sets and actions. If our primary motivation is merely to stop something that really gratifies our inner natures, I doubt if we will ever stop it for very long.

Scottie had changed. He had a different focus. He wasn't overwhelmed with the lusts that seem to preoccupy so many of us. Scottie had learned the secret of purity that Jesus prescribed in the Sermon on the Mount. Jesus set a different course of fulfillment and happiness by saying, "Blessed are the pure in heart, for they will see God" (Matt. 5:8).

Seeing a Full-Sized God

Stopping lustful habits is never a great enough incentive for changing the direction of our life. But perhaps seeing God is.

Jesus tells us in this passage that our impurity prevents us from seeing God. That's not to say that we can't see God at all, but lust creates something akin to the blinders that are put on a horse. The horse can see, but only a little. Lust is like putting on spiritual blinders. We see God, but there is a huge dimension of God that we are missing because of the blinders. Lust prevents us from seeing a full-sized God. When we put off lust, it's as if we have removed the blinders. We see so much more of God. It is vast; it is as if we have never seen God before.

Perhaps seeing God is just the motivation we need for purity. Simply to say no to lusts that gratify our desires won't do it. But when we desire God and start experiencing a dimension of Him that we didn't even know existed before, we will want more. The more we see of God, the more we will want to see. And we can't see more if we're wearing blinders.

Scottie seemed to see more of God than other people. It's as if he viewed a world that others couldn't see. I think it is because he was so pure. He had taken off the blinders.

Goose Bump Moments

Have you ever had one of those superspiritual moments? A moment where God seemed to be so close you could touch Him? Maybe you call them "goose bump" moments. Sometimes they happen in a period of worship. Other times they take place as someone is preaching the Word. Once I was a part of a revival where God seemed so close that I could just feel Him all over the place. Several of these times have happened at church when Scottie was there.

Now, Scottie and I never sat beside each other at church. He had his place by the wall on the second row of the left side. I sat on the front row in the middle. But every time I ever had one of those super goose bump moments, I would turn and look at Scottie, and he would already be looking at me. It was a unique look. He didn't look straight at me. No, he would be looking at me over the top of his glasses. He would have his big ear-to-ear grin and a kind of slyness in his countenance. He was waiting for me to look.

When we finally connected, he would nod twice. It was as if he were saying, "This is real." I felt as if he was acknowledging the legitimacy of the moment. He was telling me that I was truly seeing something. He had already seen it. Perhaps he was seeing something all along that the rest of us were missing. Maybe in his purity, he was seeing God like none of us had ever seen Him before. But every time I had one of those moments, Scottie had seen it first. Scottie was telling me in those special moments that more were available.

Peering into Heaven

Once I started tasting those moments, I wanted more of them. Once you taste God, nothing but God will do. Seeing God became the greatest motivation to say no to my lusts. Saying no wasn't enough for me to stop, but when I realized that I was missing God, I wanted to change. I wanted to see Him. And this uneducated guy with CP who could barely talk was way ahead of every one of the rest of us at church. He was seeing God. And he just smiled or laughed. He waited to see if we would see Him too.

Scottie had what I needed most. He had what I wanted most. And he helped me see the way to get there. I was willing to leave the gratification of the flesh when I had the opportunity of the glorification of my soul. Scottie was living on another plane. He didn't need the fantasies of the flesh—he was seeing God.

Scottie-ism #10
Seeing God is better than seeing whatever else you are looking at.

Some of you may be trapped on the Internet looking at sights you can't get away from. Others are lusting after a person you cannot have. Perhaps you have gratified the visual and are now moving into the physical. How do you get out of it? How do you stop when you have tried over and over again? Saying no will never be enough. If you have failed to stop time after time, you will probably fail again. You don't have enough power or motivation to stop. But once you see God, change is possible. He is not visible on the Web page, in the magazine, in your fantasy, or your afternoon affair. You can't see Him there. You have to leave the lusts behind to see what you are really looking for. And seeing God is enough to do it. It is the only motivation big enough to leave the old stuff behind.

Scottie saw more of God than the rest of us. The blinders had been removed, and he was peering into heaven. Maybe he could see the angels that we couldn't. Yes, Scottie seemed to possess a dimension of sight greater than 20/20.

One time I sang an old song with Scottie. It goes like this: "Oh, I want to see Him, look upon His face." Scottie had already started seeing a glimpse of the eternal. He was looking upon a face that was veiled to others. And the beauty of that face is better than anything else that the rest of us could see. Once you see that face, you just don't want to look back. No other view satisfies like that one. Seeing God is far better than seeing anything else. The lusts that seemed to fill us before never quite satisfy again. They pale in comparison with the glory and the radiance of seeing God.

"Blessed are the pure in heart, for they will see God."

Fellowship 11

*F*ellowship. It was Scottie's favorite word. If I ever
asked a rhetorical question like, "What does the
church need?" Scottie would always yell out,
"Fellowship!" And then there were times when I
didn't ask the question at all, and he still yelled out,
"Fellowship!"

What did fellowship mean to Scottie? I'm not
sure that I can fully define it, but it always included
the elements of people and food. Scottie didn't col-
lect a lot of possessions, but he valued experiences
with people, especially if they involved food.

Throughout Scottie's early years at the Northwest
Church, he would ride a special van that Rick

Gleason drove to the CP Center. In later years, Scottie came to church using public transportation. No matter how he got there, Scottie was supposed to return to his home the same way that he came, but that rarely happened. More often than not, Scottie would miss his ride home. As a result, he would mingle around the church building looking for a ride. And Scottie was happy with a ride from anyone. He never heard the deal about not accepting rides from strangers–Scottie never met a stranger. It could be said that strangers were only friends that Scottie hadn't met yet.

Scottie had a method for fellowship. First of all, he had to miss his ride. That was easy. Then he had to talk someone into giving him a ride home. Now that was a little more difficult. When he finally got his ride, he would tell them that he had not eaten. He had his sad story down to an art form. He would manage to get a pathetic look on his face when he was describing his predicament, and he could make you feel really sorry for him. With just a look, Scottie could make you feel all the pain and difficulties of his handicap. When you eventually asked him what you should do, Scottie would list all the restaurants in the area as possibilities. Scottie had scored.

Scottie absolutely loved eating out with people. And if he could get you to pay for it, all the better. Scottie always had money and would willingly pay, but if you even hinted at picking up the check, Scottie would never look back—the check was yours.

Scottie loved many kinds of food, but pizza was his favorite. And he loved Godfather's Pizza best of all. He would have been happy to eat every meal there. On Sunday nights, we would often have about fifty people at Godfather's after church. Nothing was more like heaven to Scottie than that pizza time.

If someone had not offered to pay for Scottie's pizza yet, he would try to find someone who would share. Why wait? He would look first for people who had already received their order. Then, he would simply sit down beside them and give them his hungry look. How could they resist? Instant pizza. Already paid for. What could be better!

Manners didn't matter when it came to pizza. Certainly, Scottie was capable of manners, but they seemed to disappear when a pizza was in front of him. Dave Altizer was the ride after church one Sunday night. As usual he ended up with Scottie at Godfather's. Dave was an intern at church, which meant that he was pretty well flat broke. Digging through his pockets, he came up with just enough money to buy a pizza. It was all the money he had.

When the pizza was set down before them, Scottie

sneezed all over it. Not just any sneeze, as you can imagine. Yes, Dave had received an extra topping for free. As he looked at Scottie, Dave only got the Cheshire cat grin. Dave was so poor, though, that he just went ahead and ate the pizza. Scottie didn't care; he knew where the sneeze came from.

Eating with his mouth open was a given. Scottie didn't do it any other way. Did he not know better? Was he incapable of good manners? No, Scottie was a please-and-thank-you kind of guy. He could learn a little etiquette if need be. But over pizza, why bother?

But the best fellowship of all was when the whole church would have one of those potluck dinners. Scottie thought they should happen every Sunday. In fact, he didn't call them potlucks, he called them fellowship.

From Stranger to Friend

Scottie had an unusual belief: You were no longer a stranger if you would sit down to eat with him. With the messes Scottie could make and the flashes of food from his open mouth, eating with Scottie could be a rather gross experience. But Scottie thought if you made it through a meal with him, you had transformed the relationship from stranger to friend. If you were scared of Scottie because of his handicaps, all you needed was a little fellowship. Sit down and eat together. That's all it took for Scottie. Then you would have a mutual experience and a better understanding of each other. You had entered his world and survived.

I think Scottie thought all problems could be solved with a little fellowship. Just get all the people who were not getting along to sit down together at the same table. Then bring out the food and pretty soon the problem would be smaller. Maybe he had noticed the opposite to be true. When people were no longer getting along with each other, he didn't see them eating at the same table.

The Last Supper

Scottie called me repeatedly during the last week of his life. He wanted to have a fellowship. I didn't know it would be his last supper; he didn't know it either. But it is what he wanted more than anything else in the world, so we had one.

Scottie's last supper came after our third service, our contemporary one. Although it was new and different, Scottie had finally adjusted to the changes. In fact, he had more than adjusted. He wasn't merely tolerating how others were worshiping. He was fully engaged. I kept hearing comments throughout the night like, "Will you look at Scottie!" He was in a zone. He was worshiping God with no holds barred. His face looked as if he was seeing another world. His voice was stronger and louder than ever before. He wasn't on pitch, but he had quite a joyful noise going.

When the service was over, we went to our Family Life Center and ate. Then we ate some more. Scottie was thrilled. He kept telling us that the food was making him sick, but he ate it nonetheless. Obviously, he wasn't feeling very well, but it didn't matter to him. It was fellowship.

As usual, Scottie missed his ride. He didn't want to leave that night. He stayed until the last person there had to take him home. He closed the church building down. It was about 11 P.M. when Scottie finally headed home.

We never saw him alive again. He died that night. He had his last supper. He went out in a blaze of glory (Scottie's style). His last night was the best. Worship and fellowship. Nothing could be better.

We gathered in the same room where Scottie had his last supper for his memorial, and I gave Scottie's eulogy. All of us were a little teary eyed as we recalled the story of a very loved Scott Callis. Then we passed a microphone around the room. Dozens of stories were told. Most of the stories were about Scottie using my name or a crazy experience over a meal. As the stories progressed, we couldn't stop laughing. There wasn't a person in the room who hadn't been conned out of a meal. All of us had fallen for the same lines from Scottie.

In a few moments, the little guy had become larger than life. We cheered for our hero. We applauded our friend. We concluded that if he had known it was the last day of his life, he wouldn't have changed a thing. He spent his final hours doing what he loved most and what he considered to be most important. He worshiped. He ate. He spent time with his friends.

Then we all went to Godfather's Pizza to celebrate his life. It wasn't my last supper, but I wanted to eat it and share the food and the moments with the people around me as if it were.

Scottie-ism #11
Eat with people as often as you can. And eat like it's your last meal. It might be.

Fellowship Like Jesus

Have you ever noticed how often Jesus eats with people in the Gospels? He eats with His disciples. He eats with his friends at parties. He eats with His enemies. He eats with new followers. He eats with outcasts.

When Jesus paints a picture of the kingdom of heaven, over and over again He uses the image of a banquet feast. The kingdom is depicted with people and food, and everyone is invited. The people who were frequently overlooked (like Scottie) were invited, and they came. The kingdom was about fellowship. Scottie was trying to experience a glimpse of heaven on earth. Do you blame him?

Indeed, Jesus was a little bit like Scottie. Or should I say it the other way around? By His own example Jesus told us that something special happened when people ate together. Problems often got solved. Relationships got formed. Walls and barriers came down.

Scottie knew he was different. He knew people had a hard time with handicaps they didn't understand. But he thought if you would eat with him, things would change. Maybe you would experience fellowship. It took some effort to spend time with Scottie, and he knew it. You had to carry the pizza for him. You had to ask him to repeat his sentences dozens of times. You had to take a napkin to help him clean his face. And if he had to go to the bathroom, well, that was a lot more than you wanted.

It took some work to have a meal with Scottie. But if you went through it all, you had an experience, a few laughs, and probably a good story or two. Scottie knew that any relationship with him took some work on your part. He thought that if you took that kind of effort with any relationship, it would have to turn out better. Of course, he's right. All relationships take work.

The early church had a meal called the agape feast. It was a love meal, a fellowship. It seemed to be a vital part of the life of the church. Perhaps the Lord's Supper was even taken in this meal until the Corinthian church abused it. Paul told the church that if they couldn't have fellowship at this meal, then they should forget the feast and simply have the Lord's Supper.

Most churches today don't abuse meals like the Corinthian church did. We simply have diminished the meal's importance in our time together. In the book of Jude, years after the letter to the Corinthians, the agape feast had survived. Maybe we should bring it back. Perhaps we could understand our differences and build relationships better if we ate more frequently together and worked at loving each other more.

The Bible tells us that two things last forever. In Isaiah 40:8 we find that God's Word lasts forever: "The grass withers and the flowers fall, but the word of our God stands forever." In John 5:28-29 we find that people last forever: "Do not be amazed at this, for a time is coming when all who are in their graves will hear his voice and come out—those who have done good will rise to live, and those who have done evil will rise to be condemned."

Scottie seemed to know the importance of this. He devoted himself to the two things that last: God's Word and people. Although he couldn't read, he looked at his Bible every single day. And he devoted himself to people by prioritizing his relationships above anything else.

When I look at Scottie's life, it is an indictment of my priorities. His life may have been simple. He may not have had the highest IQ, but he got his priorities right. If there is one thing I have learned from looking back on my Sundays with Scottie, it's that I want to change my priorities. I want my life to be more like Scottie's. I've learned something: I want more fellowship.

I've decided that I'm going to quit eating alone so much. I've experienced too many fast food meals in the car by myself. I'm going to eat with my family more. I'm going to eat with my friends more. I'm going to eat with my church more. I'm going to fellowship.

Do I have regrets in my life? Yes. I regret that I haven't spent as much time as I could with the people I love most. I have had too many anonymous meals. I have done too many meetings and been too many places that may make me feel important but where I didn't experience fellowship.

I'd like another meal with Scottie. I would even pay for it. I might not even complain if his mouth was open when he chewed. I miss him.

I'm going to go eat with someone I love today. Or maybe I'll go find someone strange to eat with. And maybe that meal is all it will take to make me love them. And perhaps I will find love in return.

If you ever hear me ask, "What does the church need?" please say, "Fellowship."

Mascot

*S*cott Callis died early on a Monday morning. He never knew how old he was. I was told that he was forty-six, but his mom told me he was forty-one. Surely she would know.

He was not only survived by his mom, Thelma, but also by his brother, Stephen. Scottie loved his family dearly. Scottie's dad had preceded him in death by only a few weeks. As a result, death had been continually on Scottie's mind, but not his own death.

Scottie's death was a total surprise to everyone. He was at church Sunday night. My wife, Barbie, and others told me they had never seen Scottie praising the Lord more. That's saying a lot because

Scottie loved to praise the Lord. He had told me several times that he wanted to have a fellowship (meal) this weekend, but he kept telling me it was going to make him sick. He just said it would be "no good." Scottie thought he was having problems with his stomach that week, and it was really his heart.

Scottie was the mascot of the Northwest Church. Now that might sound derogatory at first. But let me explain. In the Northwest there are colleges in Oregon that have ducks and beavers as mascots, cute and small figures. And Scottie was cute and small. But that is not what I'm talking about. I'm from a school that had a man dressed in black with a red cape riding on a black stallion as a mascot.

When I was at Texas Tech, I was a part of a frater- nity called Saddle Tramps. We were a service fraternity that helped a lot with the various sports at Texas Tech. We were responsible for the mascot—a black stallion— Happy V. It was our job to transport this beautiful horse to Memorial Stadium in Austin for our big football rival- ry. As a group of Saddle Tramps spent the night in Brady en route to Austin, the Cowboys, the counterpart to the Saddle Tramps at the University of Texas, allegedly found us. Evidently, they had been following our group. And we were absolutely unaware of it. That night they snuck in and painted our black stallion their school color—burnt orange. And Happy V couldn't breathe through the paint and died.

I was sad. I was mad. Something big was gone. It was as if the whole university had been violated. Now the mascot isn't the essence of the university. No, the school is really the students, the faculty, and the educational philosophy; yet, this horse was the symbol of it. When the horse ran onto the field, we remembered what was good about Tech. It united us. We cheered together. We were stirred and motivated.

Now the essence of the church is Jesus. But Scottie was somewhat like a mascot; he symbolized what was good in our congregation. He reminded us, motivated us, and united us around what was good.

People Who Care

In the late '70s, our congregational leaders got together to set some goals. One was "to be known as a church who cares." But we said that wasn't a proper goal. How could we measure it? How would we know if we had ever accomplished it? But we let it fly, and it was published as one of our goals.

To our surprise one day, we got a measurable answer to what seemed like an immeasurable goal. *The Seattle Times* wrote a full-page article about our congregation with photographs and called us "a church who cares." Why? Because of the cerebral palsy ministry at the Northwest Church. Included with the article were pictures of some of our wonderful members with CP like Ila Mae, Duane, Mike, and Scottie. Certainly there was the temptation to brag because we were recognized as a caring group, but that never happened. No, that is not the point of the CP ministry. The people with CP are the ones who truly taught us how to care. We all knew that we had learned more from Scottie than he had learned from us.

Well, we got another horse. Even got one for that very game at Memorial Stadium. But it was never quite the same to me. I kind of missed the old one that died.

To this day in my mind and heart, I can go back to Jones Stadium and remember standing there on the track around the football field waiting in anticipation for Happy V, looking for that black stallion to run out of the tunnel and onto the field. I can still feel the emotion of it, and I will always remember. There were other stallions, other mascots that ran out of that tunnel, but none for me like Happy V.

Remember

As I stand in the front of the sanctuary of the Northwest Church in Seattle, I will always remember a man in black who walked down the aisle with a clank,

clank, clank. There will be other people who walk down that aisle, but none for me like Scottie Callis. He was our mascot. There will never be another for me like him.

It's good to remember. After the Israelites had defeated their dreaded enemy, the Philistines, Samuel set up a big rock that he called an Ebenezer. It meant, "Thus far has the LORD helped us" (1 Samuel 7:12). Samuel wanted them to remember. He wanted God's people to remember every time they traveled by that spot that God had helped them there. When they saw the rock, they would remember.

Scottie liked to talk about old times. He would often just say, "Remember." Because of our close relationship, that's about all that needed to be said. I would remember.

I've been told that spiritual defection usually starts with a lousy memory. You simply forget what is important. Or maybe you forget who is important. When Jesus confronts the church in Ephesus with losing their first love in Revelation 2, the first thing that He tells them to do is to remember.

I teach preaching at a nearby Christian college. Recently I received a letter from one of my former students, Danny Chamberlin. He reminded and honored me in a thank-you note and models well the point of remembering people:

I often think back to my last year at college. I remember that you encouraged me to change my major from youth ministry to preaching. I thought that was odd since my preaching was so poor. But when I began to preach regularly here I sensed God's power and favor, and especially His grace as I proclaimed His Word. . . . I just finished my master's program and realized through that process that I am who I am because of the people who have invested in me. I know that seems so obvious, but I have forgotten how true it is. I say all that to say this, thank you for investing in me and raising the bar in my life.

Scottie-ism #12
Remember. Don't ever forget the people who have made you who you are. Keep something of theirs to remind you of them.

I've kept Scottie's crutches. They are still there at the Northwest building, right where he used to put them when he sat in his familiar pew in the amen corner.

They are an Ebenezer. When I see them, I remember. They sometimes make me melancholy, but usually they make me smile.

When I went to Scottie's room, there were all kinds of little things scattered around the room to remind him of me. Pictures. Orange golf balls. Sermon tapes. There were more things in his room to display me than him. I was his friend, and he wanted to remember me.

We are who we are because of the people who have touched us along the way. Don't forget them. And thanks for helping me remember Scottie with this book.

You probably want to know more about how Scottie died. He simply went to bed that Sunday night and didn't wake up Monday morning on this side of the world. No one did an autopsy. We were told that his heart malfunctioned. I wish I could tell you more, but that's all there is to it. He lived simply. He died simply.

Catherine Marshall tells the story of her husband, Peter Marshall, speaking at the Naval Academy on the day Pearl Harbor was bombed. Marshall, the chaplain of the U.S. Senate, delivered an incredibly timely sermon especially since he had not yet been made aware of the attack. His text came from James 4:13-14: "Now listen, you who say, 'Today or tomorrow we will go to this or that city, spend a year there, carry on business and make money.' Why, you do not even know what will happen tomorrow. What is your life? You are a mist that appears for a little while and then vanishes."

To these young people who would soon be entering a war, Marshall expounded on what death was like. He told a touching story of a young child who was terminally ill. When the child asked his mother what death was like, the mother asked her child if he could remember nights where he had fallen asleep in her mom and dad's bed. But when morning came, he awoke in another bed in another room. How did he get there? During the night, his father picked him up in his loving arms and carried him to the bed in his own room.

Marshall explained that this is how death occurs. We fall asleep in one bed and wake up in another one. In reality, we fall asleep in one world and wake up in another. How did we get there? Our loving heavenly Father carried us there.

In his younger days, Scottie couldn't walk. He had to be carried a lot. His father was often picking him up to take him where he needed to be. For years, Scottie had to be laid in bed.

So how did Scottie die? Is there a better explanation than this one? He fell asleep in bed one night and awoke in a different place. How did he get there? His Father carried him. When he awoke, it was a new morning. Scottie was in a new place. The best place of all—heaven. And there was only one thing that his Father neglected to bring. Yes, Scottie's crutches were left behind.

Notes

1. Jim Morris and Joel Engel, *The Rookie* (New York: Warner Books, 2001), 40.

2. Charles Swindoll, *Three Steps Forward, Two Steps Back* (New York: Bantam, 1982), 14.

3. Stephen Lundin, Harry Paul, and John Christensen, *Fish!* (New York: Hyperion, 2000), 107.

4. Viktor Frankl, *Man's Search for Meaning* (New York: Simon and Schuster, 1984), 12.

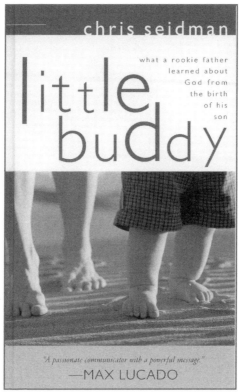